Poetry in Black and White

By
Michael Ray King

Photography by
Ella Forrest

Published by
ClearView Press Inc.
PO Box 33431
Palm Coast, Florida 32135

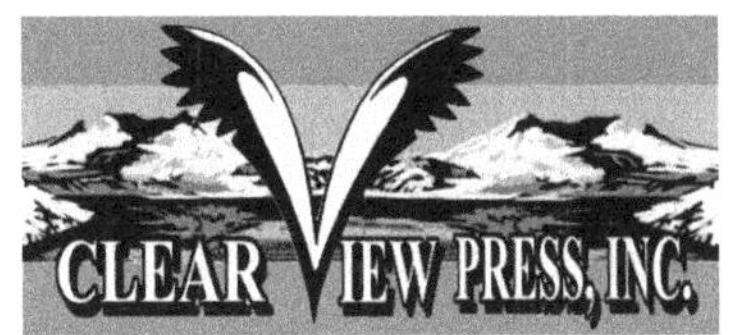

Poetry in Black and White

By Michael Ray King
Photography by Ella Forrest
Except Pages: 8, 10, 14, 26, 76, 96
Photography by www.dreamstime.com

King, Michael Ray
Forrest, Ella
ISBN 978-1-935795-72-8
LCCN 2011941991

ClearView Press Inc.
PO Box 33431
Palm Coast FL 32135
www.ClearViewPressInc.com

Printed in the United States of America

Table of Contents

Poetry in

Black and White

Dedication

To the people in my life who pick me up from the sadnesses that try to keep me down and to those who bring joy and smiles sincerely given.

To Ayesha, for your midnight heart, may you always embrace your dreams and aspirations.

A special thank you to Ella who has a keen eye and Cindy who keeps the details running smooth.

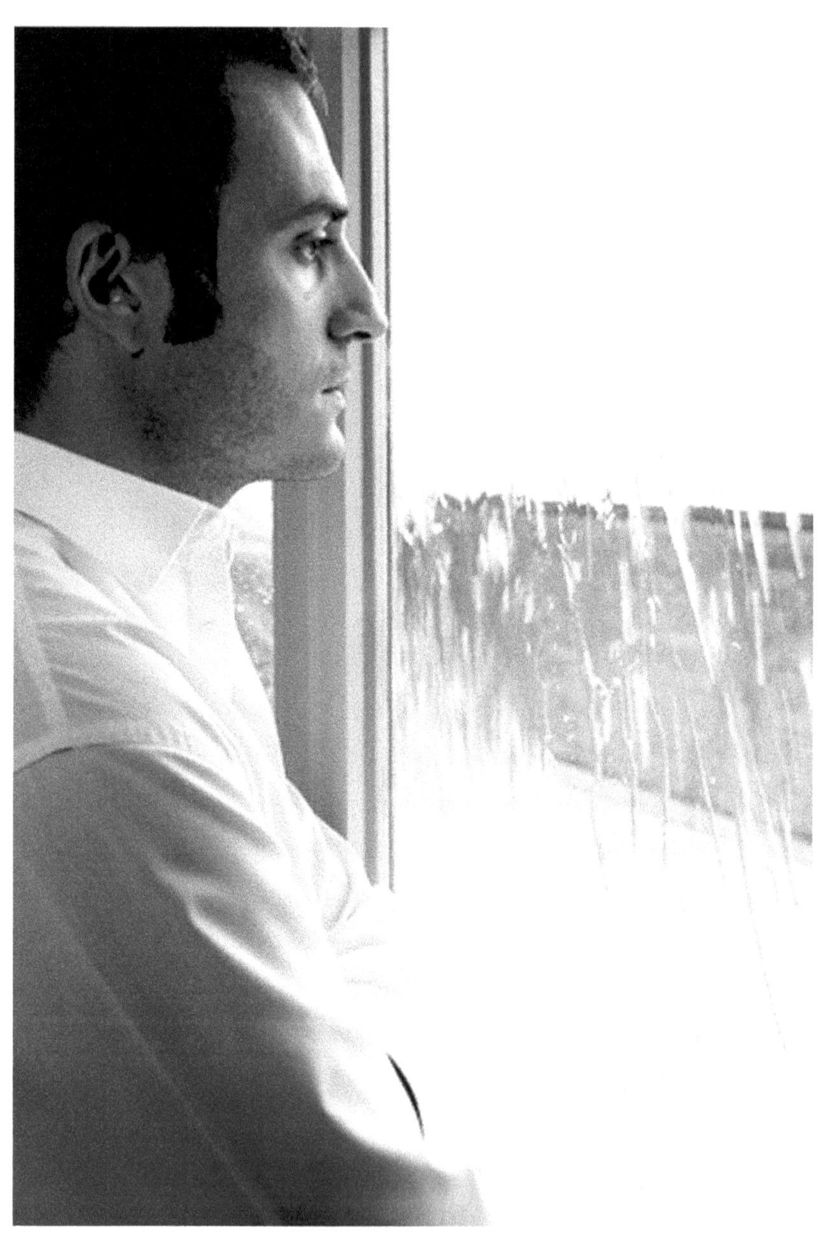

West Virginia Rain

Soft West Virginia rain cascades through my spirit

Gentle droplets brush a lush emotional landscape

Sadness mixes with joy

Solitude from melancholy to peace

Soft West Virginia rain defines my heart

Life-giving and placid, home and friends

Tranquility wafts through a calm drizzle

Cares of the world no longer pierce my mind

Soft West Virginia rain tugs at my soul,

Whispers pleas to stay my feet

West Virginia rain mends me whole

I wonder at how I could ever leave

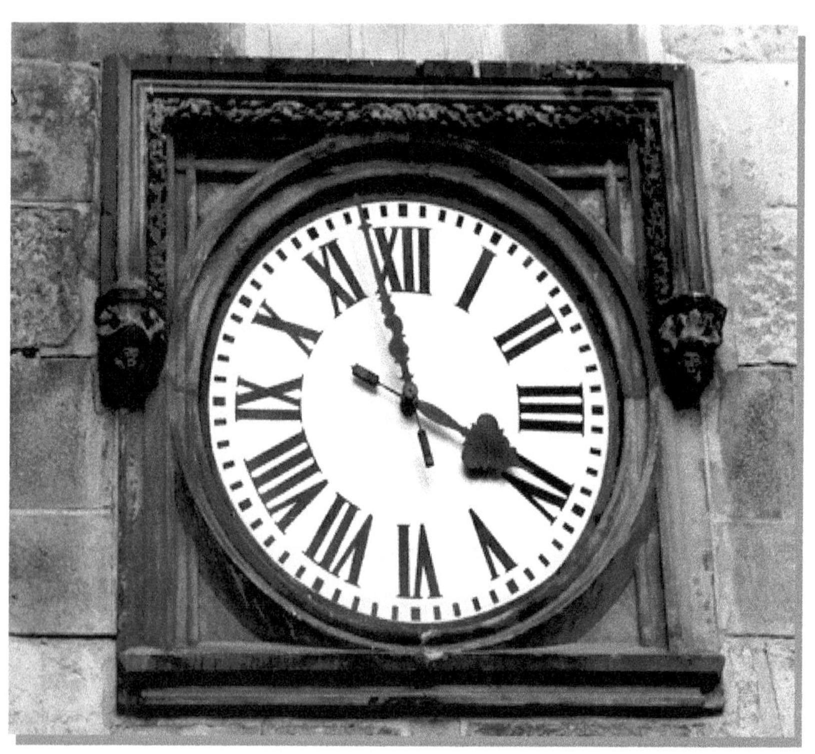

Time in Life

There are times in life, like,
Sitting by an old oak tree.
I feel the love
She holds for me.

There are times in life
Lying in bed at night
Waiting on those bright head lights, and,
Her voice.

There are times in life,
Breathing in sacred silence,
Dreaming lazy contemplations,
When she sashays through my soul.

When comes the time,
Where all the days are right,
All the nights ease in, and
We revel in each other?

Why do we choose
Our work, all that's pressing,
Over what we value most
- each other?

There are times in life
When I need to love my wife.
That time is ever-present
Like now.

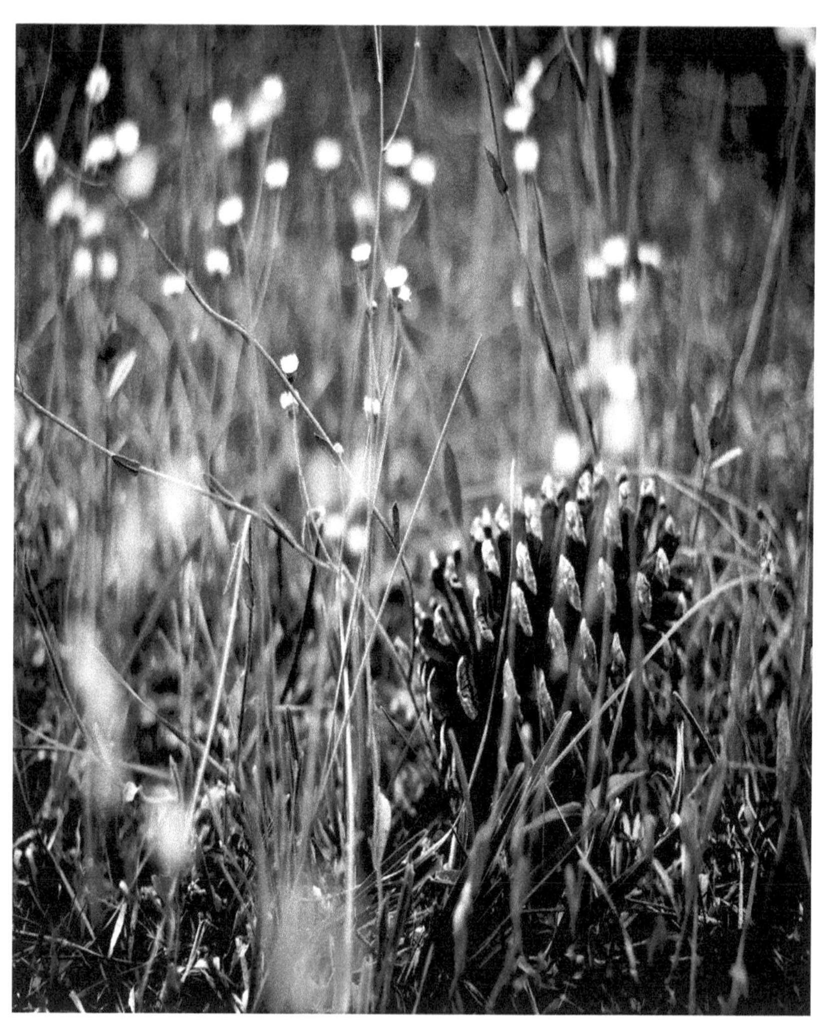

A Love For All Seasons

Blue skies, silken afternoons
Autumn leaves – dance around you.
Winter nights, glowing fires
Silver snowflakes – flirt around you.

Spring flowers, bright fresh air
April showers – laugh around you.
Summer meadows, cooling shade
Radiant sunlight – sparkles around you.

My love, my dreams,
My life – revolves around you…

All for which I live.

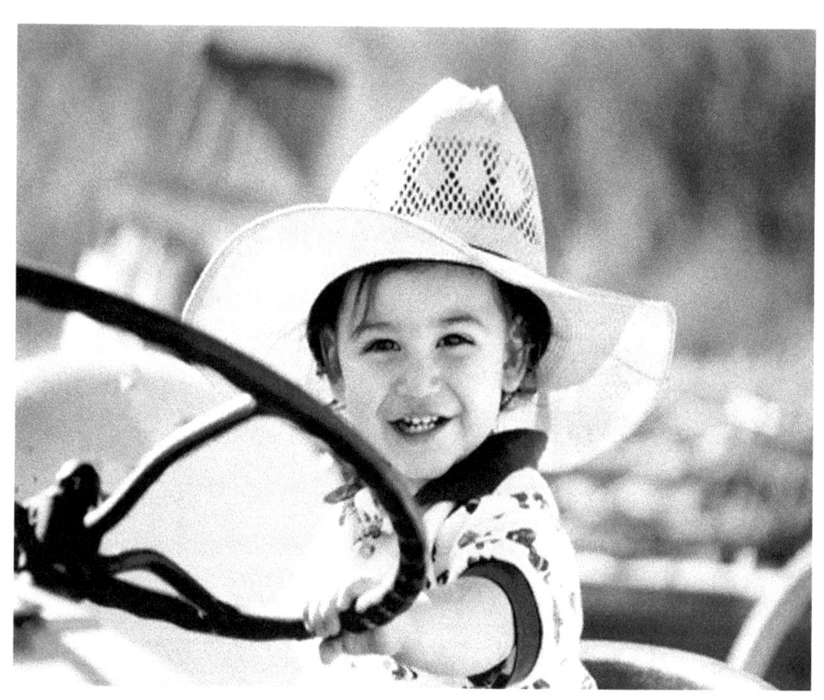

The Smile

Innocent boy smile
Five years a sunbeam,
Lover of life and big trucks,
Carefree heart-stealer, son.

Dark night hovers forever,
Boy, smile, sunbeam,
Sees no night, only trust,
Safety in his small, loving world.

Dark night hovers forever.
Bright confidence in those around him,
All laugh and giggles and smiles.
Dark cloud, disguised blood, descends.

Bonds of blood and home,
Little boy smile believes.
Evil worms a filthy path to the smile.
Sunbeam that cured the world - extinguished.

Innocent boy-smile, stolen.

Calloused, malevolent spirit.
Blood taboo not enough to stay evil's hand.
Wicked, vile, despicable, cruel, hateful, soulless.

Dark night hovers forever
Innocent boy-smile crushed. Broken.
A life now consumed by hate. Anger.
Yet, remembered is the smile the demon stole.

Tears will never heal it.
Time will never return it.
Precious five years of innocence not enough
To overcome the hand of Satan's spawn.

Dark night hovers forever
Innocent boy-smile lives in my heart.
I beg God himself to return this smile.
Beyond the only life it knows – in my heart.

Not enough…

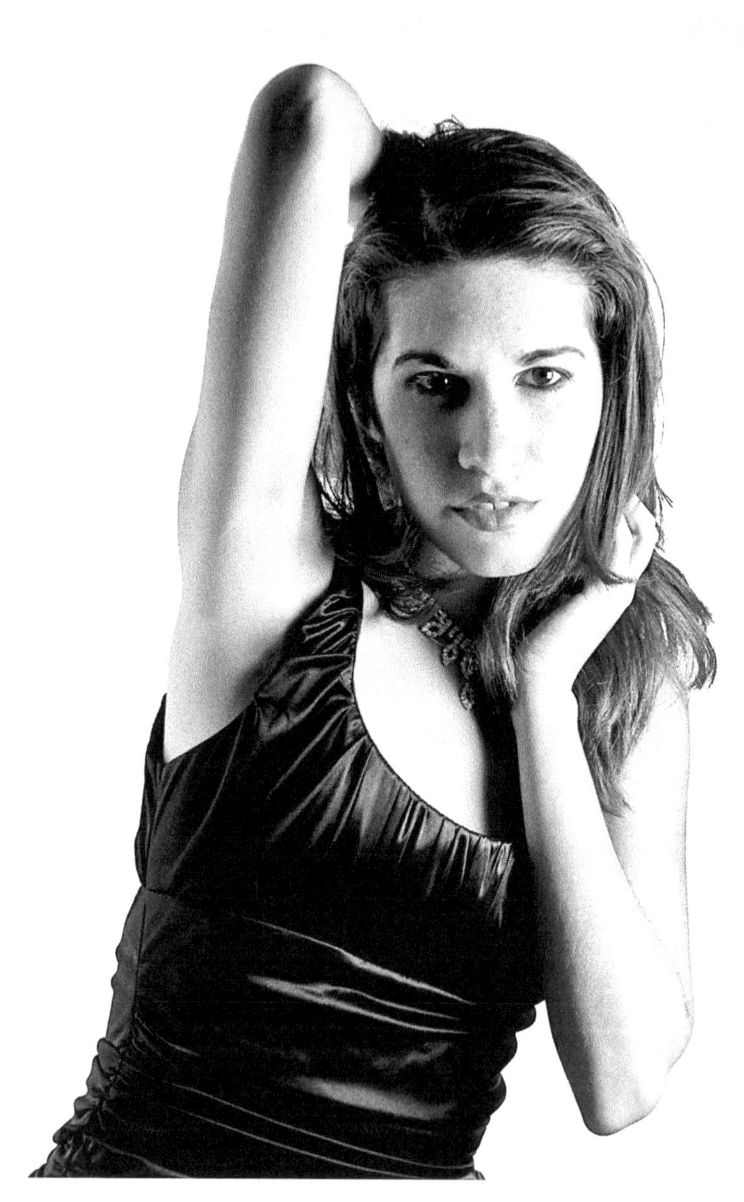

The Sketch

Door opens. Soft brown eyes smile.
Hallway. Table. Notepad. Pen.
Mona Lisa blushed and ready.
Pen at rest. A hand extended.

Petite and lithe.
Dark hair. Waves of thick silk.
Hand travels up her milk-soft arm.
Shoulder. Neck. Ear.

Second hand mimics the first.
Her neck leans back,
Eyelids fall, ecstasies paint her vision
Hands descend to the curve of her waist.

Slight pressure forward with one hand,
Back with the other.
Bodies locked. Lips rain on each other.
Release behind the eyelids.

Separation. Chairs. Pen. Hand.
Frantic scratches on paper.
Curves and lines squiggled.
Pen down. Both stand - eyes wide.

Hands again.
Buttons tucked. Released.
Cleavage. Hand tremble.
Eyes still locked.

Stop. Palm pointed to the unbuttoned.
Pen in hand. Scratches. Squiggles.
Clank. Fingers back to the task.
One shoulder bared. Next, a blouse-plummet.

Hands to her back,
Four eyes wistful.
Clasps released. Fingers trail slowly,
One strap dropped. The other.

Palm again. Scratches. Squiggles.
More frantic, less structured.
Clank. Delicate flesh cupped.
Caressed. Kissed. Turned.

Hands under arms, return.
Hot breath over her shoulder.
Ear heated. Heart raced. Skin tingled.
Her chest rises – falls – with heightened frequency.

Back arches into him.
Neck on shoulder.
Eyes again view the panoramic flow
Across eyelids electrified.

Another turn as a shirt floats the ceiling.
Chest against chest. Lip on lip.
Passion on passion.
Four hands track two backs.

Separation. Palm. Scratches. Squiggles.
Another palm. Pen, paper – extracted.
Jet-fluttered to a corner.
Hand found. Led to couch.

Notebook, corner heaped.
White paper snowdrift,
Dotted by black-scratched words,
Another unfinished literary work of art.

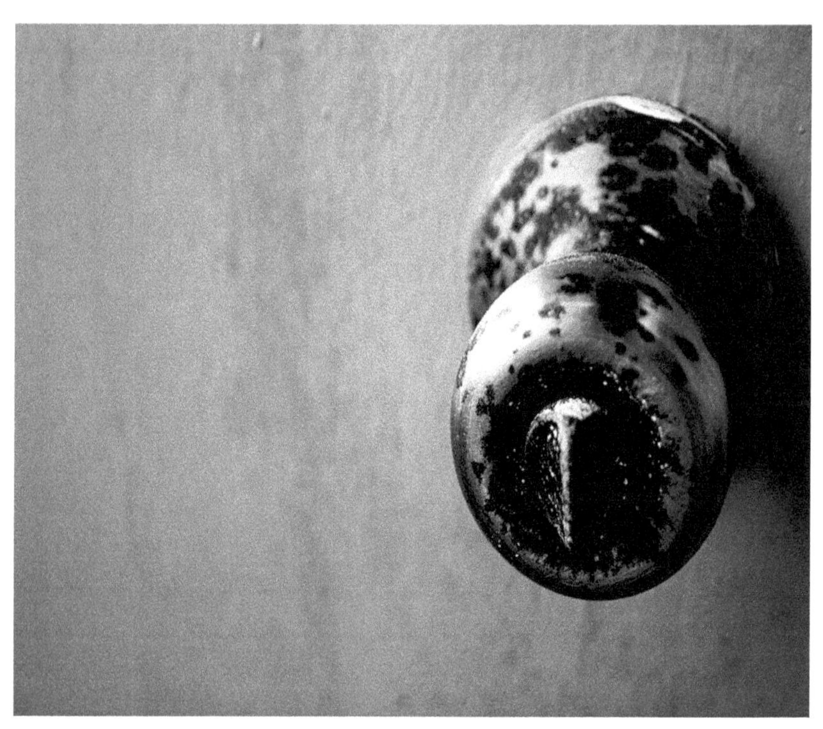

The Chill Wind

A chill wind that rattles bones
Alone on midnight-darkened streets.
Alone, save for rustling leaves
Alone, save for anguish.

Once the chill settles in
Warmth becomes a distant dream
A lie to torture as soon as believed
A hope crucified in the soul's core.

Choices made. Mistakes as well.
Shivers all that remain.
Wracked vestiges of dreams' death throes
Meaningless now to everyone.

Who shall care of destruction?
Sisters and children and mother?
Not the father who never understood his role.
Not the women who knifed and stabbed every good thing offered.

All that's left shakes into stillness.
Suffer the chill wind that rattles bones
On midnight-darkened streets of loneliness and solitude
And the knowledge existence will never be the same again.

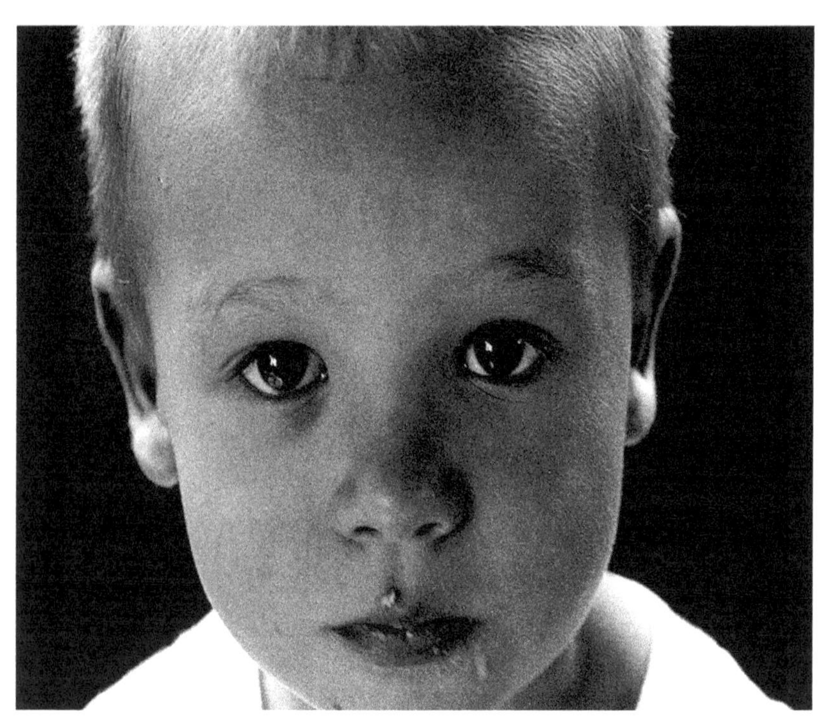

Mining Green

Succulent, ripe, but, is it not green?
A berry plucked when thought unseen
Finger now a globulous mess
Lumpy and sticky and tough to confess.

A graveyard search for an unseemly prize
Furtive guilty glances knife from eyes
Undersides of tables, of desks and of chairs
Draws forth the finger if only he dares

Strong bonded glue to harden and dry
Nestled in secret, no view of the sky
Finger, rolled clean of despicable remains
Slithers back, more treasure the cavern contains

Satisfying connection to the next chunk of clay
Skilled finger adept at work and at play
Mined well and prized like well refined sugar
A finger-filled trophy, the well-rounded booger.

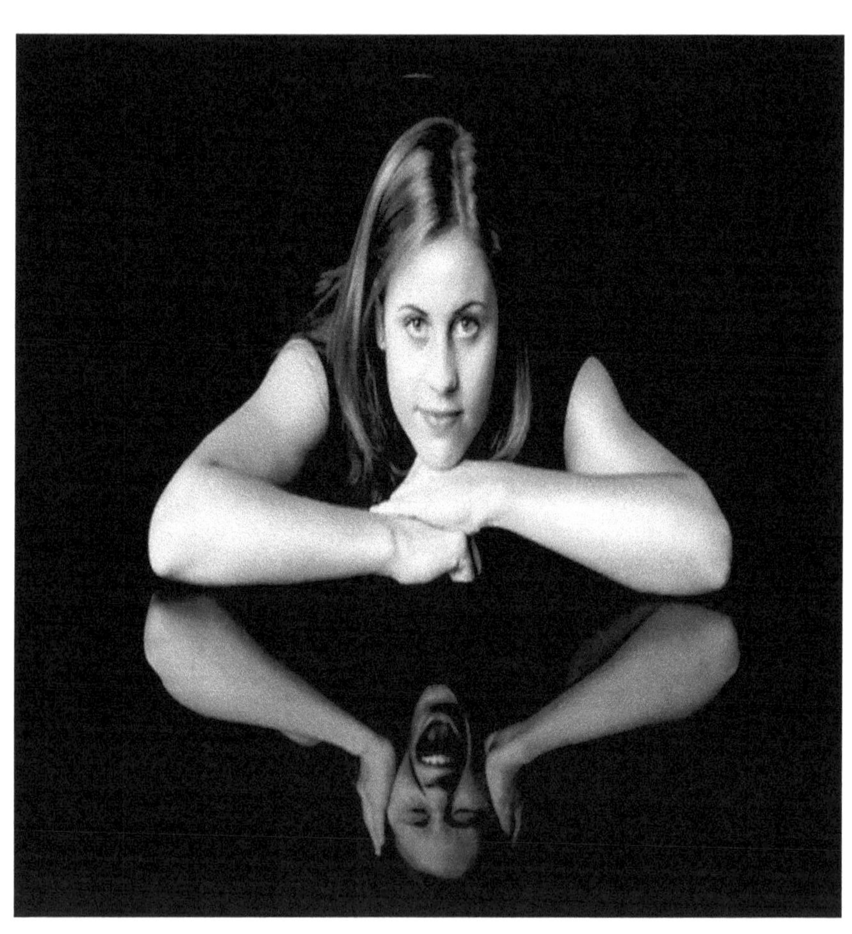

Superficial Acquaintance

Never ask what it's like to dive in the shallows,

To struggle to be the person others say you should be.

Desire stumbles to dance the rhythms of life, but

Flails on wind-whipped surfaces

Dreams and ideals remain below, while

Mystic, siren voices call. Your heart pursues the flute,

Yet panic-charged feet sail away.

Sinister, echo-guided dreams weaken your will.

Never ask what it's like diving in the shallows.

Mirrors elicit no more than silent pain.

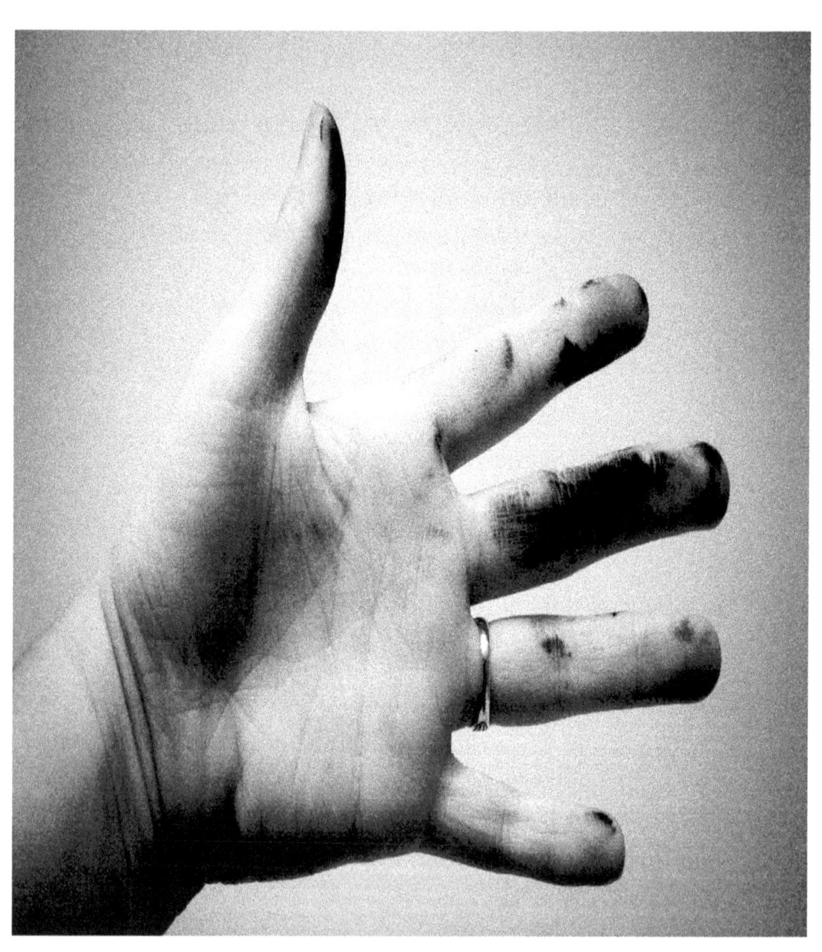

Stolen Heart

Each day draws nearer the launched ship
She must watch leave.
Each tepid night recalls her sweet lips,
Never our pair to meet

Never to be the one who says yes
Never to fall from grace with God
Desire may rest only in faded memories
Eternal of its own accord

A heart in no way free
In time she will cease to see.
Recognition the two could never be
I'll live with a stolen heart

Honor weighs heavy in life
Especially in a woman's eyes.
Stroll humble from her electric touch
Her silent departure – my unheard cries

A heart never to be free
In time she will cease to see
Even though we could never be
I'll cherish a stolen heart

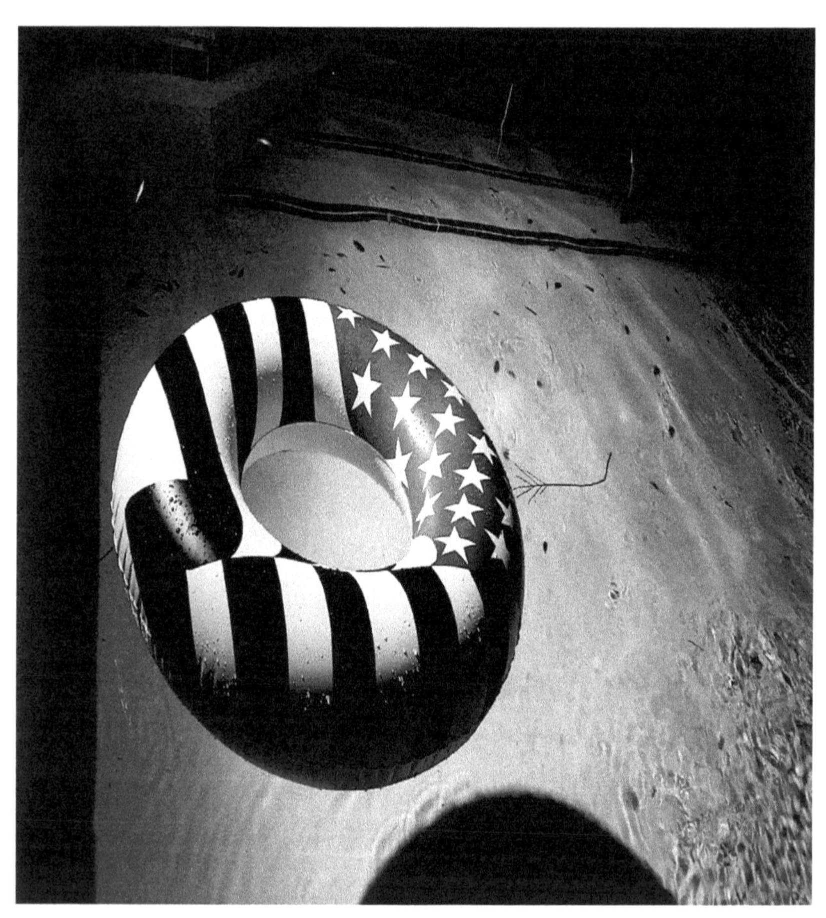

Society's Demise

Stilted rasps in darkened halls
Free-range pain, corporate thralls
Dark diamond hearts fear return
Pit wasted fools writhe and burn

Ideas once aloft, prim and new
Beliefs bright, fresh, glinted dew
Run through muck, disdain, scorn
Now lie wicked, broken, shorn

Nobility lost, no man's gain
Sensibility shattered, splintered, insane
Where lies peace and love and hope?
Nothing remains but trial and cope…

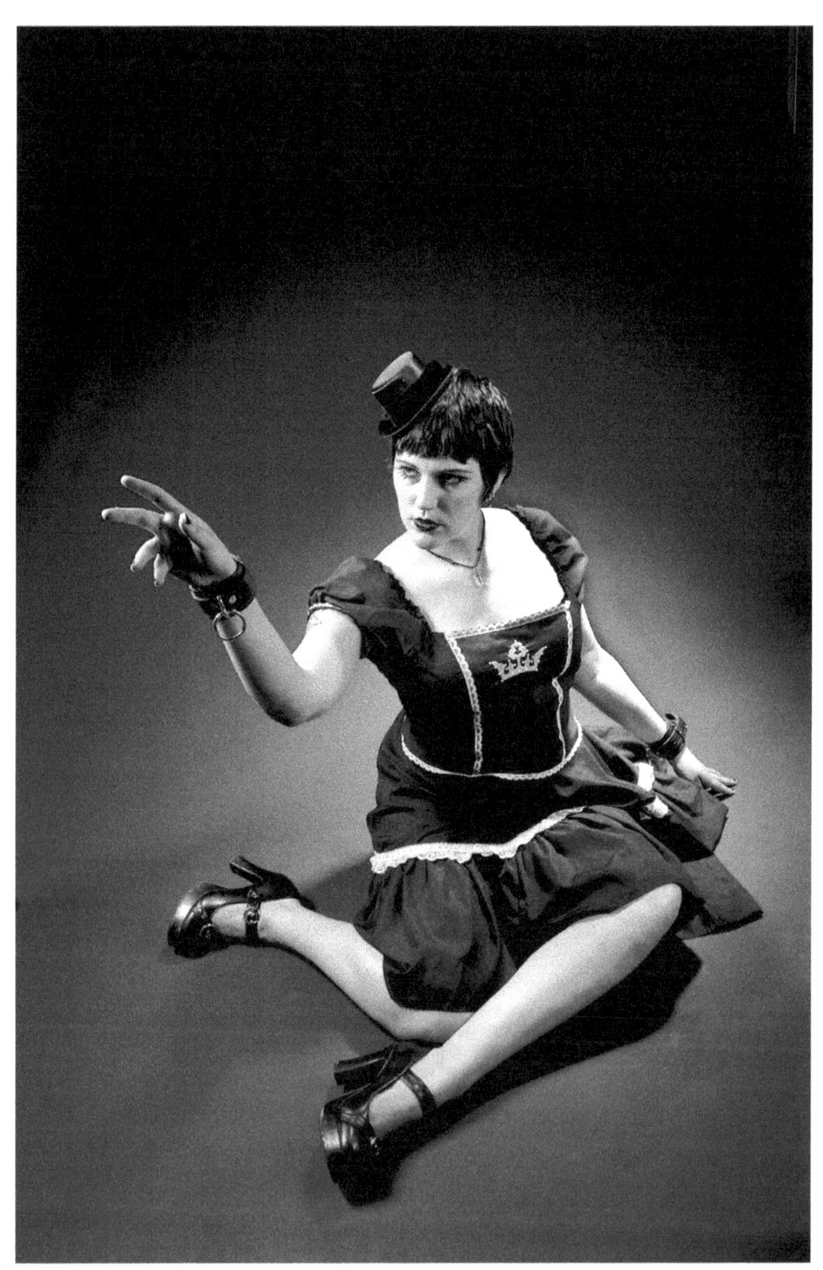

Troubled Soul

My world crumbles.
Lights on.
Clutter.
Shoes.
Easels.

You stab me with your truths.
I long for touch.
Kisses.
Attention.
Love.

No longer will my heart bleed.
Hopes.
Fears.
Longings.
Lusts.

Soul-death and detachment carve my wounds.
Gouged.
Cruel.
Uncared.
Undesired.

Impossible for love to fire unsullied.
Unbidden.
Unshorn.
Collaborative.
Fresh.

Empty vows of colorless nights.
Soulless.
Callous.
Arctic.
Isolated.

What one day passed for dreams
Now lies as molten fodder
Crafted disaster's manifest destiny -
A rubble of fabrication, deception and folly.

Era ended with no beginning
Seasons change with no reprieve
I die each night you abandon my heart
Lay to rest my troubled soul.

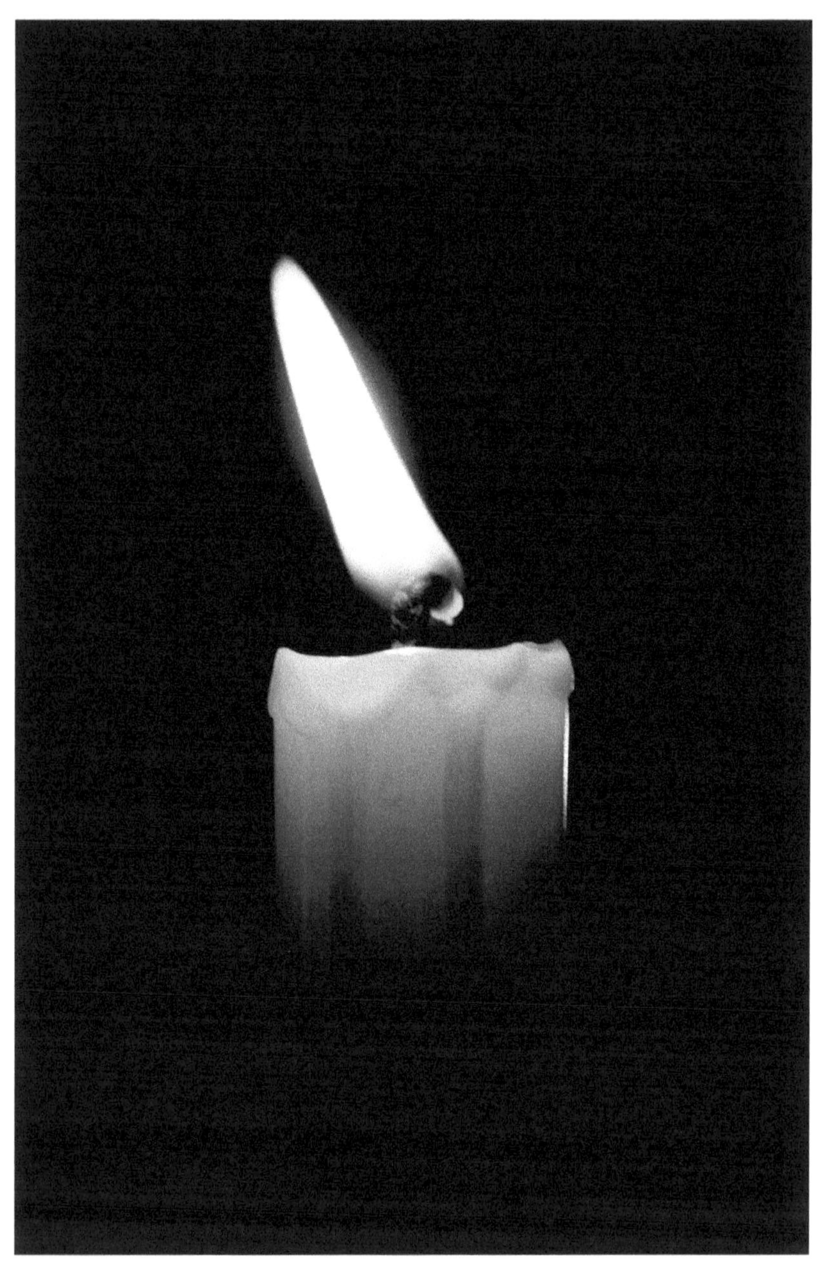

Snowbound Serenity

Slipping, sliding soft silken snow sheets

Sipping cider, scorching, searing

Seeing stores' short stockpile sold

Siren soliloquies

Send silly signals

Saying "sit still"

Soothing scene

Steals show

Sigh.

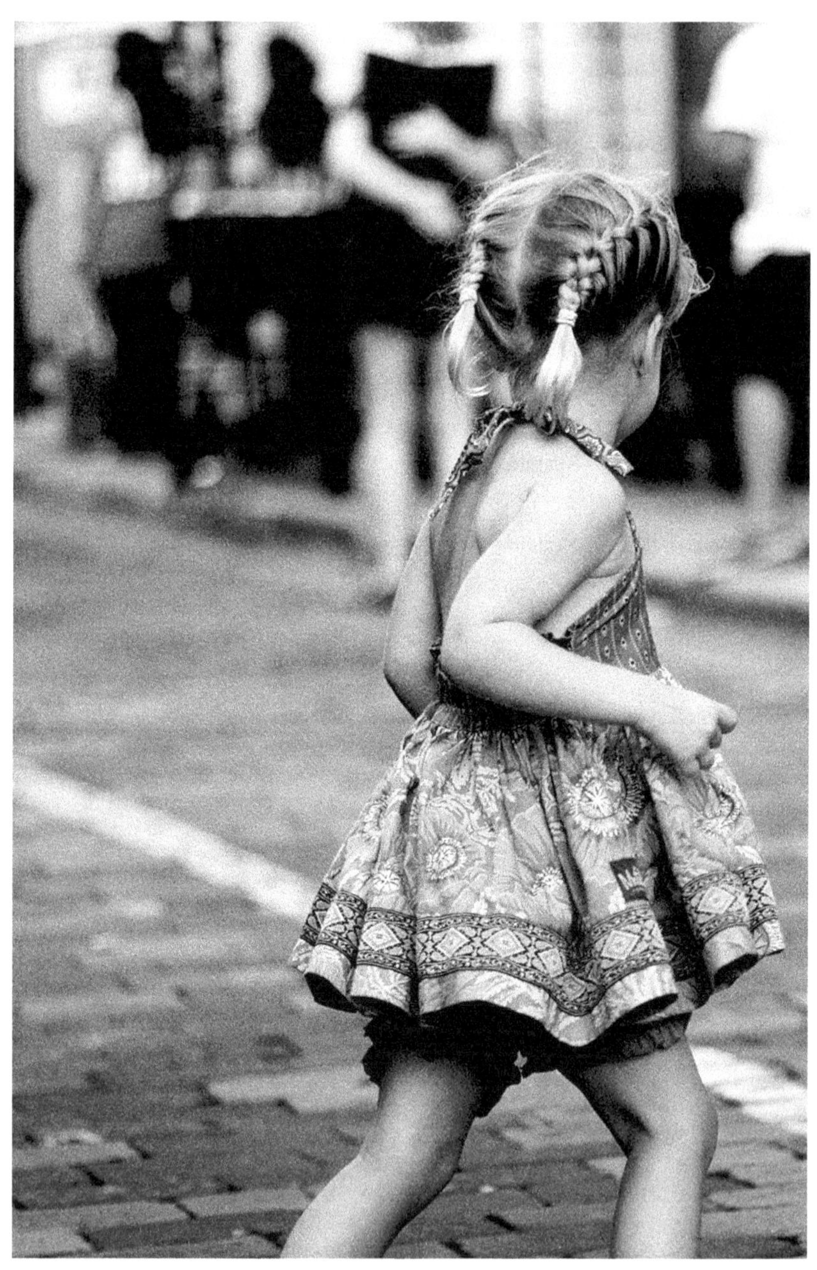

Little Girl Lost

Shrill venom. Hand-branded, crimson face.
Confused tears. Lung-ripped breaths.
Shirley Temple countenance. Little hands shaken.
Hushed little voice,
"Please love me."

Targeted, missile words
Tiny life against heavy hands.
Porcelain body. Discolored skin.
Diminutive voice,
"Please love me."

Scream pierced, hole-bored trust.
Solitude wept in perplexed anxiety.
Snake-stranglehold hands. Love emaciated.
Petite voice,
"Please love me."

Haughty vitriol, she crouches and cringes,
Little girl lost. Wandered eye-mists. Phantom protection.
Disoriented, bruised heart
Minute voice,
"Please love me."

Unforgivable callousness. Withered faith.
Young dreams crucified at conception
Meat fists. Dungeon life reinforced.
Frail voice,
"Please love me."

Lovely lass. The haunt that lingers in
Unknown smiles and unbrightened eyes.
Crushed existence reduced to flight.
A fragile voice once begged,
"Please love me . . ."

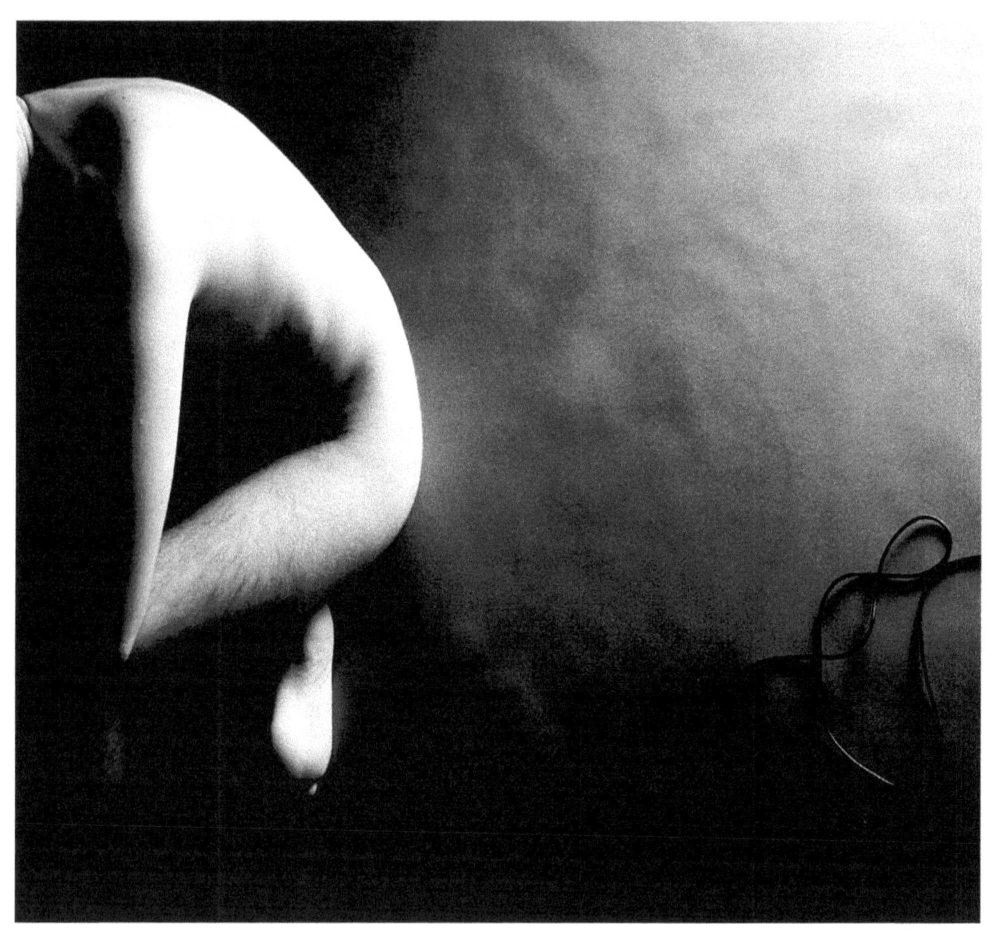

Pissed Off Poetry

I search for images I'll never find
I cranny out vestiges of cracks in my mind
I struggle to winnow every detail
I search, I cranny, I struggle, I fail

My mind sows its own oats.
My mind stretches reason,
Knows no boundaries,
No end and no season

But for the thoughts it so ably procures
For love of the craft each finger endures
Insults of rhyme in each new line
Ineptitude, fallacies, ownership – mine.

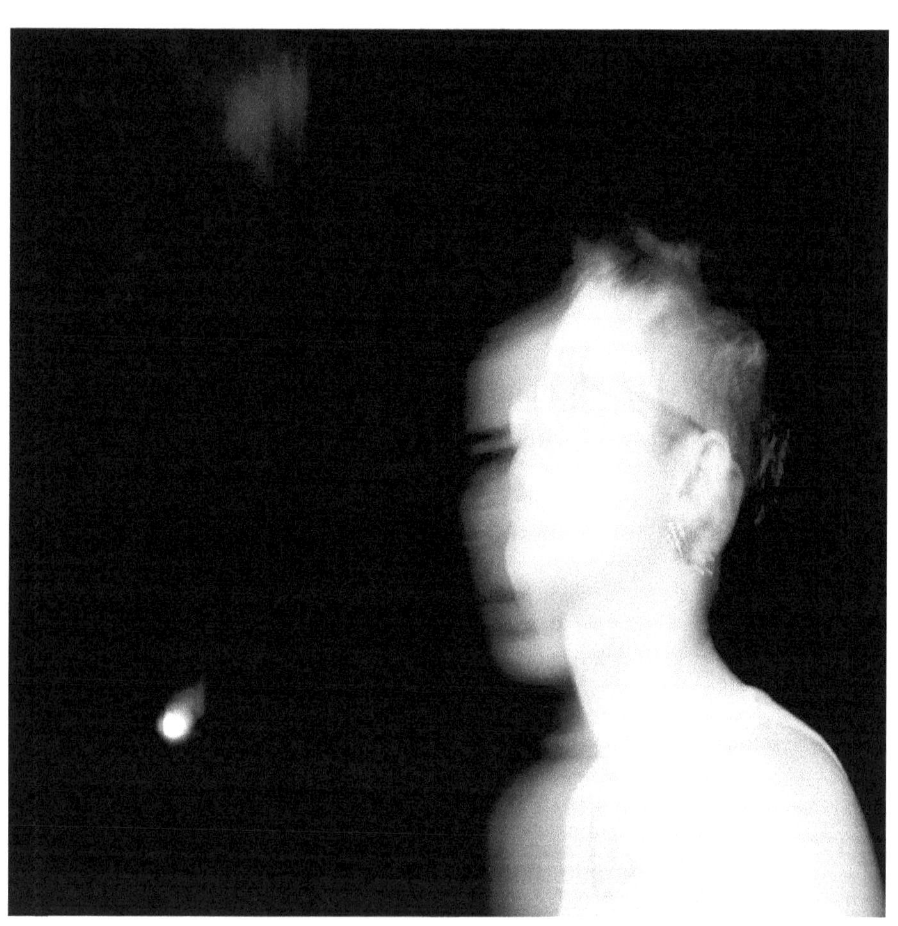

Night Writing

I mutter at sniffles
Push back the pain
Pull out the keyboard
Put on the strain

Peek over a shoulder
Resolve falls behind
Roll up the shirtsleeves
Battle the mind

Fear oncoming age
Yet full speed ahead
Stumble on fortitude
Wander to bed

Death hovers near
Hangs high in the night
Presence made known
Enchantments, foresight

Why bother to care
I wonder and dream
Until nothing is left
Or so it would seem…

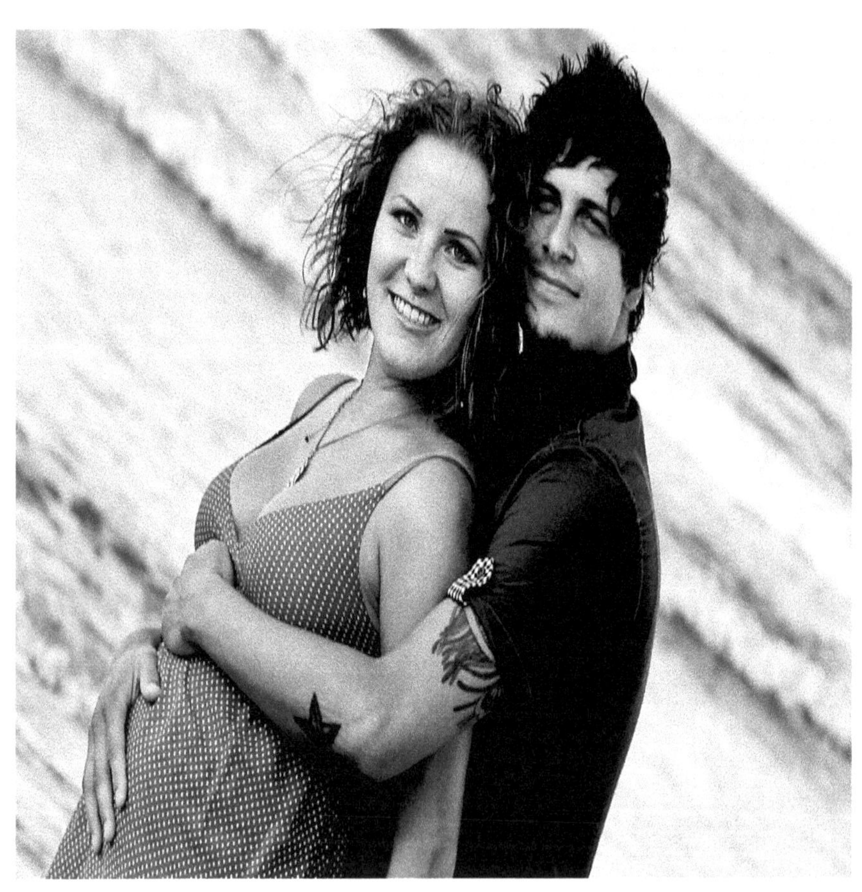

My Love

Wing to me the stars in a teacup,
Or the moon in a wicker basket.
Dapple me with golden droplets of the sun.
Sprinkled, pristine and silken, in a scarf of love.

Reveal breathtaking depths of the universe
As a backdrop for the tapestry of life.
I will know you understand then
How much I love you.

Seed me treasures lost long in the deep
Loan me your smile for a single day
Regale me with songs of tears and joy
Whisper words that soar my spirit.

There, will I say,
Reside the first blushes of spring -
My soul blossoms
At mere contemplation of your name

Christen the winds with flames of desire
Shout for the tempest to engulf me
For when you abide in my life and my heart
There is no will that is mine.

My Gentle Friend

Hollow faith, hollow heart
Follow a callow, whimsical dream
See each day melt greens to grey
Feel each night slip away

Stop with the lame-ass rhymes already
Nothing stands here for me but salt
Pillars of the faithless I must leave behind
Someway, somehow to settle my mind

Stop with the lame-ass rhymes I say
Treachery of the mind - forestall this day
Nemesis of rhyme and meter and lilt
Return to me endings that feel jagged and spilt

Rhyme forces its way into every life
Nothing completes these stanzas of strife
Like a rhyme that signals this train's at its end
Be kind to my writing, she's my true, gentle friend.

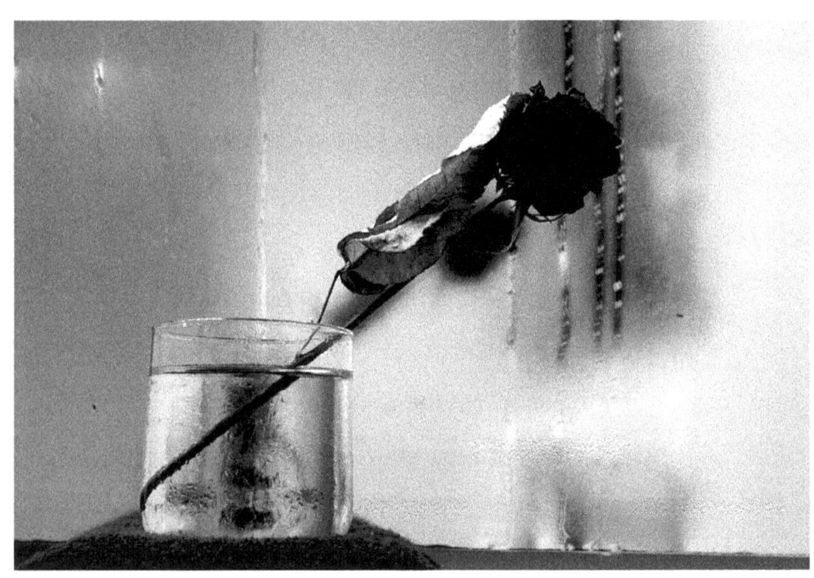

Midnight in Her Heart

Midnight in her heart:
Soft padded steps along serpentine paths
Murky light betrays a blackened world
Yet sure footwork on her trek through life.

Midnight in her heart:
Questions, so many questions, of
Why must we live this way?
Answers, so few answers, to move her along.

Midnight in her heart:
Open wound of caring,
Tears hitchhike words of kindred spirits,
Elixirs to satisfy the pain of this world.

Midnight in her heart:
Still beating firm and comforting others,
Her own damage borne of shadows and ilk,
Salved for her next foray into dawn.

Midnight in her heart:
Defies and defines beauty, love and caring
Defies them because often she gets trampled
Defines them because she can do nothing less

Midnight in her heart:
Realm of light and love and clarity,
Resurgence of that which draws her strength and
That which many adore.

May peace befall the midnight in her heart.

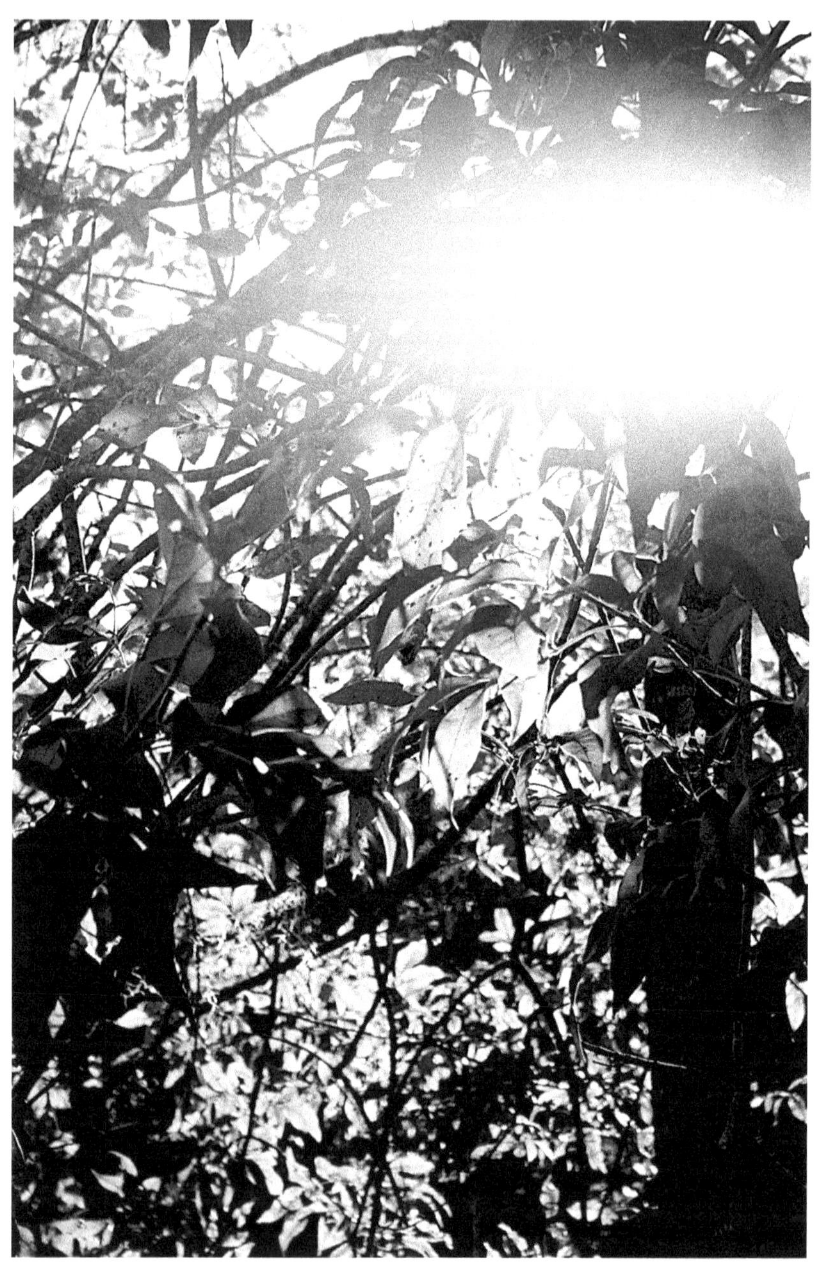

Love Songs

I could write you love songs

Star sentinels pin-stuck to the night sky

I could write you love songs

Clouds herded through a full-moon night

I could write you love songs

Tree shadow blankets on colorless grass

I could write you love songs

Heart taps your shoulder, begging a dance

I could write you love songs

Though I know you don't feel them

I could write you love songs

Every breath of every minute of every day I'll ever live

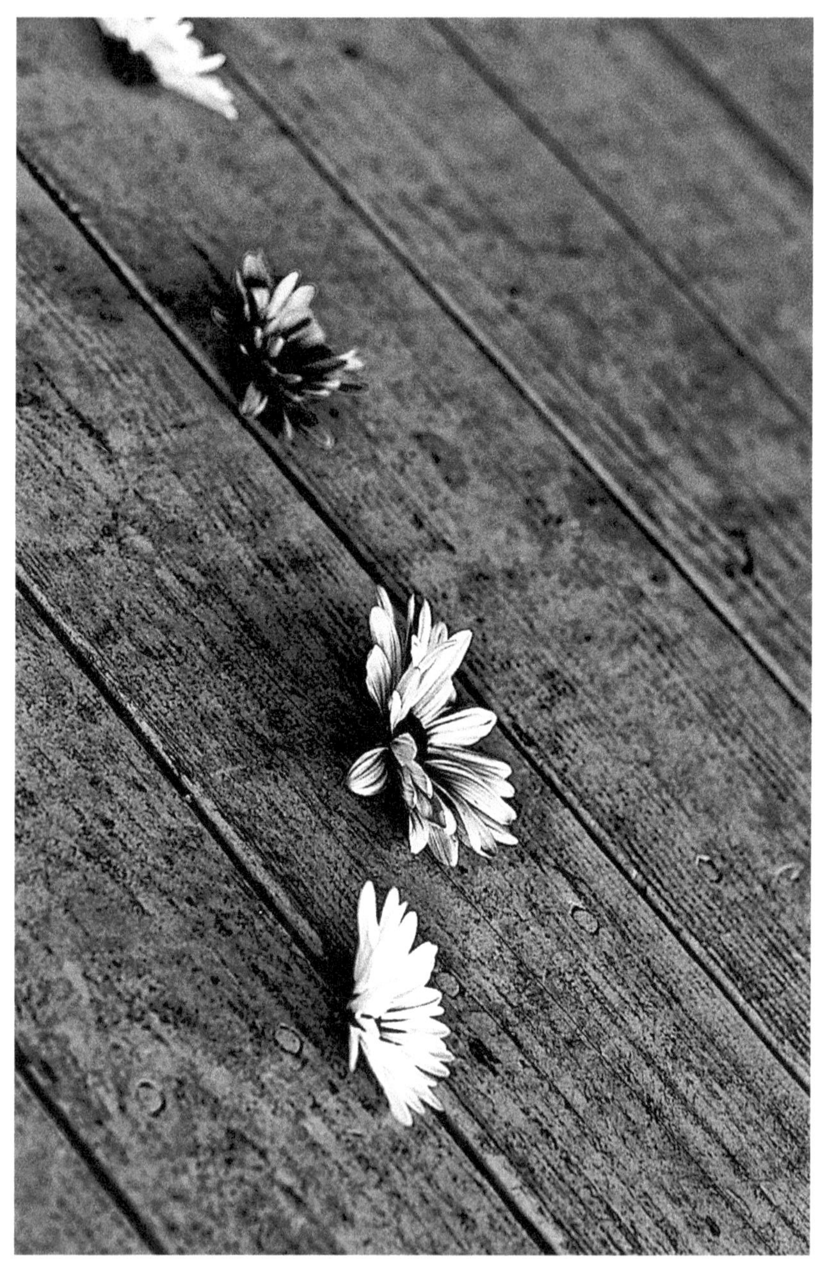

Love Is Female in Gender

Water in a rippling pool,
New-fallen rain, wind blowing cool.
Rampaging fires of love and longing,
Reach up from depths for want of belonging.

Mysterious lady, you control the night,
Veils of fancy, evasion of light.
You walk in the shadows, you skirt through the room.
Where is your black cat? Where is your broom?

Bracelets of silver fall at your wrists.
Shadows and darkness your prerequisites.
I know what I want, I know it is you.
Won't you give me your love? Give me what's due?

I chase you down alleys and find that my feet
Cannot keep the pace, can't keep the beat.
I really do crave you, and, do I dare?
Reach out with my heart, commit to care?

That's when you have me, that's when you turn.
That's when I catch you, that's when I burn.
I knew what I wanted, I knew it was you.
Did I get what I asked for, Or receive what was due?

Love is female in gender.
Maybe that's why love is so tender.
It is definitely why love is so cruel.
She brings you her mystery.

She leaves you a fool.

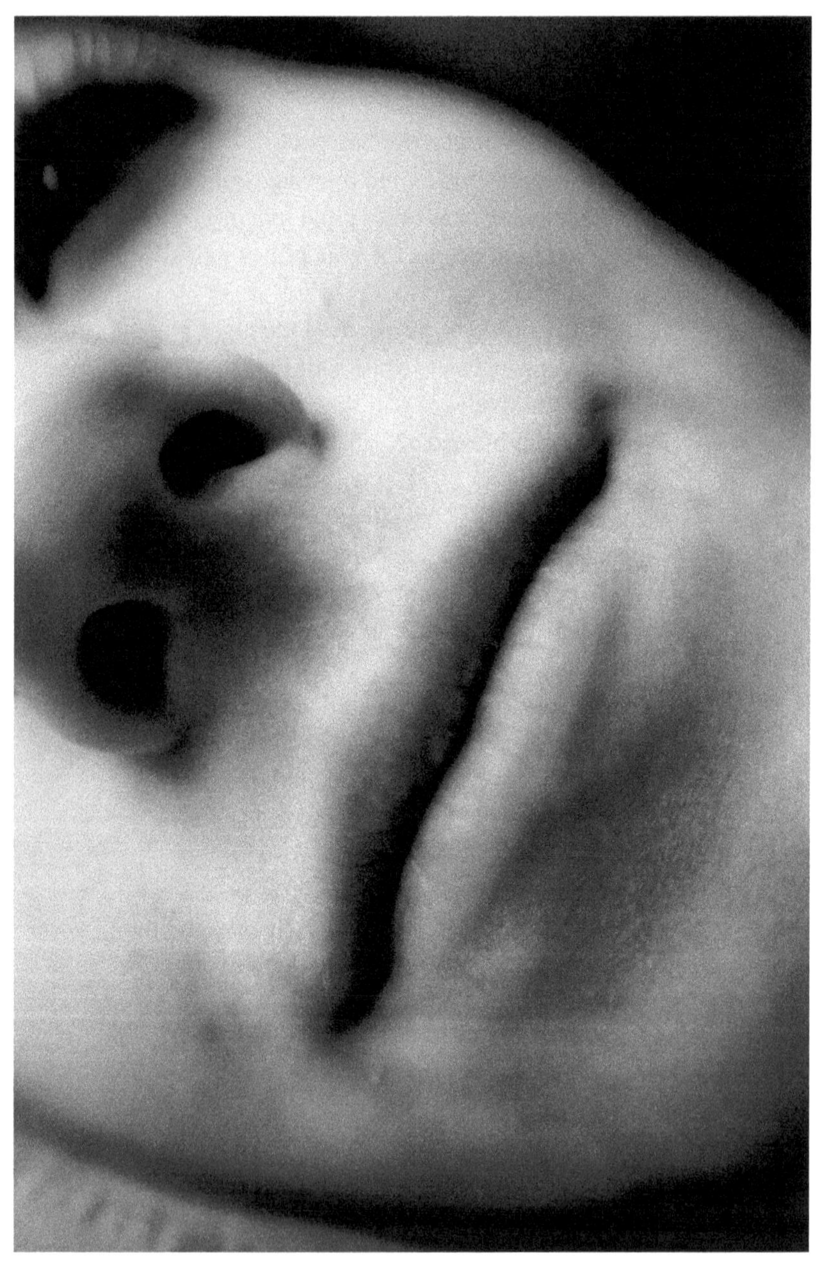

She Whispered

She whispered
"My heart soars whenever you touch me."
She lay there
Beauty, resplendent, sublime.
She whispered
"I love you always, forever and now."
I lay there
Stunned, freed, bewildered – "she's mine."

She whispered
"I need you, my breath, my love and my life."
She lay there
Beauty, resplendent, my wife.
She whispered
"Forgive me your suffering, your pain."
I lay there
Stunned. Bewildered. Translucent tears rain.

I'd long whispered
"My heart soars when we touch."
I'd lain fallow
Decades, beauty to rust
I'd whispered and shouted
"I love you forever."
I'd shared
"I need you more than my heart."
I'd murmured
"Forgive me, allow me to love you."
I'd lain there
Mystified, perplexed and confused.

Until the day she whispered
"My heart soars when you touch me.
I need you, my breath, my love and my life
I love you always, forever and now."
I cried the day she whispered
We begin over now…

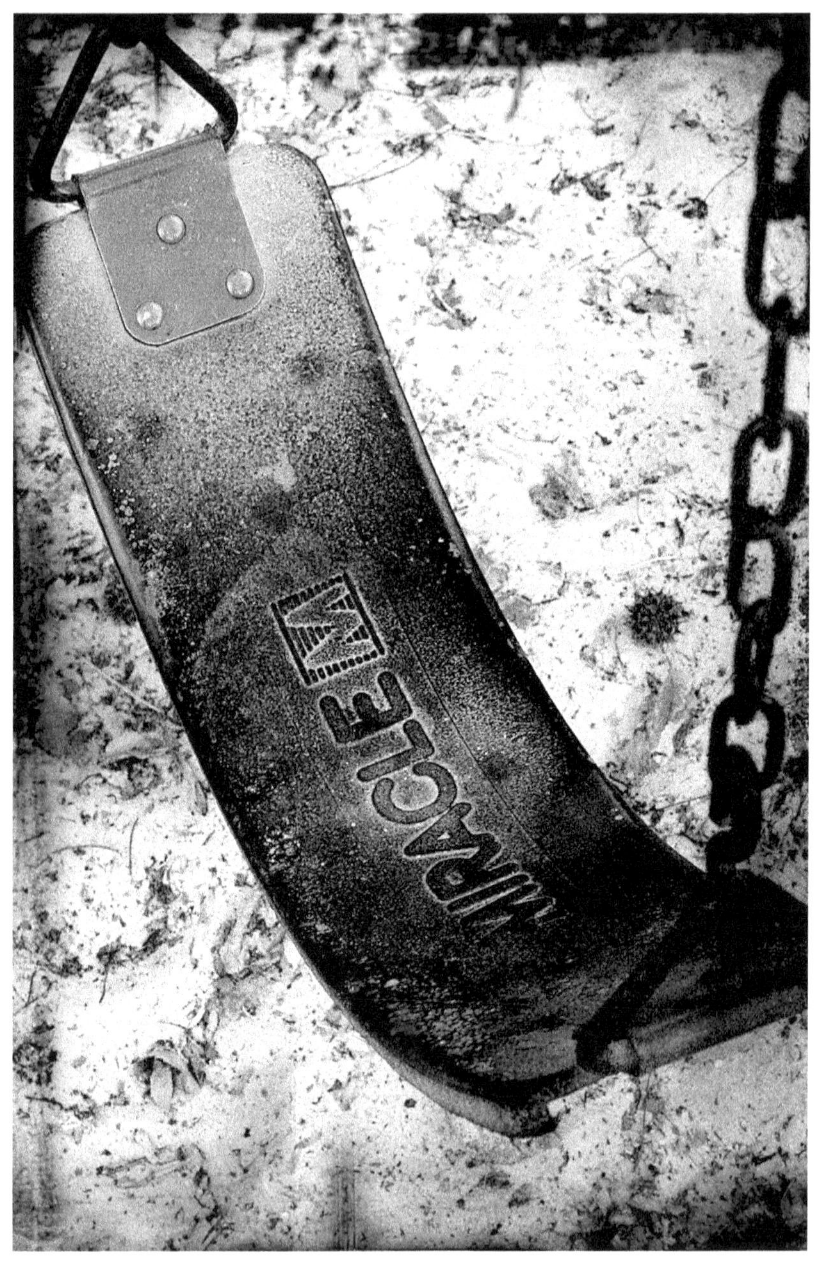
MIRACLE

I’ve Been Here Before

I’ve been here before
Far too many times
Emotionally crushed by
Callous hearts who simply did not care.

My investment in the need for them
Desire for their love and trust
Bankrupt my soul because
I gave all I had to give.

I’ve been here far too often
No man should suffer so
Weakness, no doubt, on my part
Yet a travesty of justice nonetheless.

Never let it be that
Love holds the scales of justice
For she will surely bend these weights
To her own fickle views of fate

I’ve been here and languished
For the last time
With the weak promise of tomorrow,
The only thread of life that remains

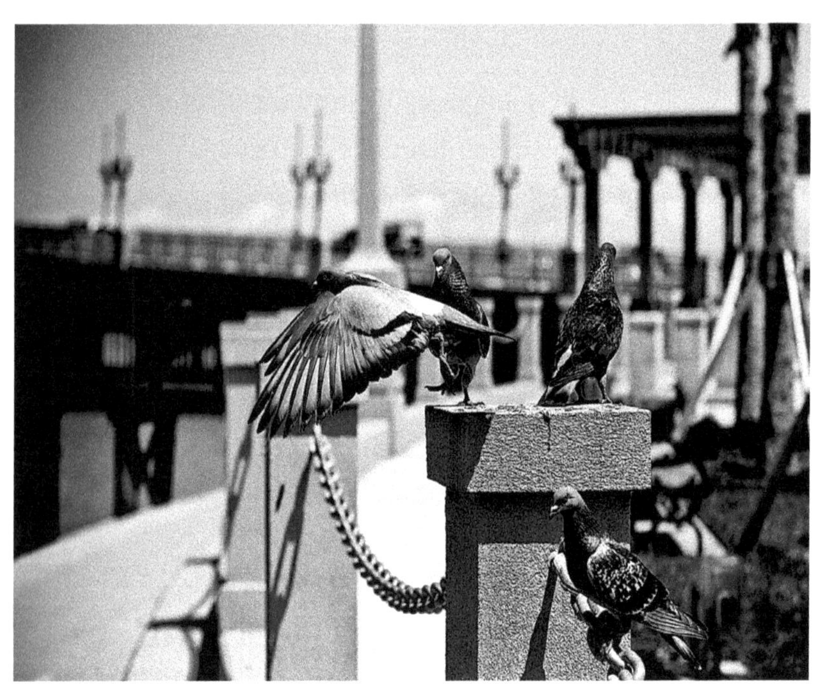

I Can Do This

I can do this.
I can find myself again.
Collect the remnants of who I was
Gather the ashes of love's cruel pyre
Rebuild my shattered heart and live again.

There will be those who don't understand,
Who question who I've become
Wonder that my metamorphosis is destructive, selfish.
But I know. I know.
I know the truth.

I know I need to move on.
I know I must step through the veil,
The veil of destruction.
The veil of upheaval and annihilation,
Into the arms of inner peace

Where this peace takes me
Will define my life.
Where my joy leads
Surely brings questions with it,
But the answers are mine.

I was down.

Crushed and discarded.

Now, hunger beckons me on.

Hunger for life. Feeling. Joy.

Accompanied by a callous disregard for those who would deny me this.

I can do this.

Reinvent my passions.

My love. My hope.

I will rise, cast off the ashes,

To live once more and smile again.

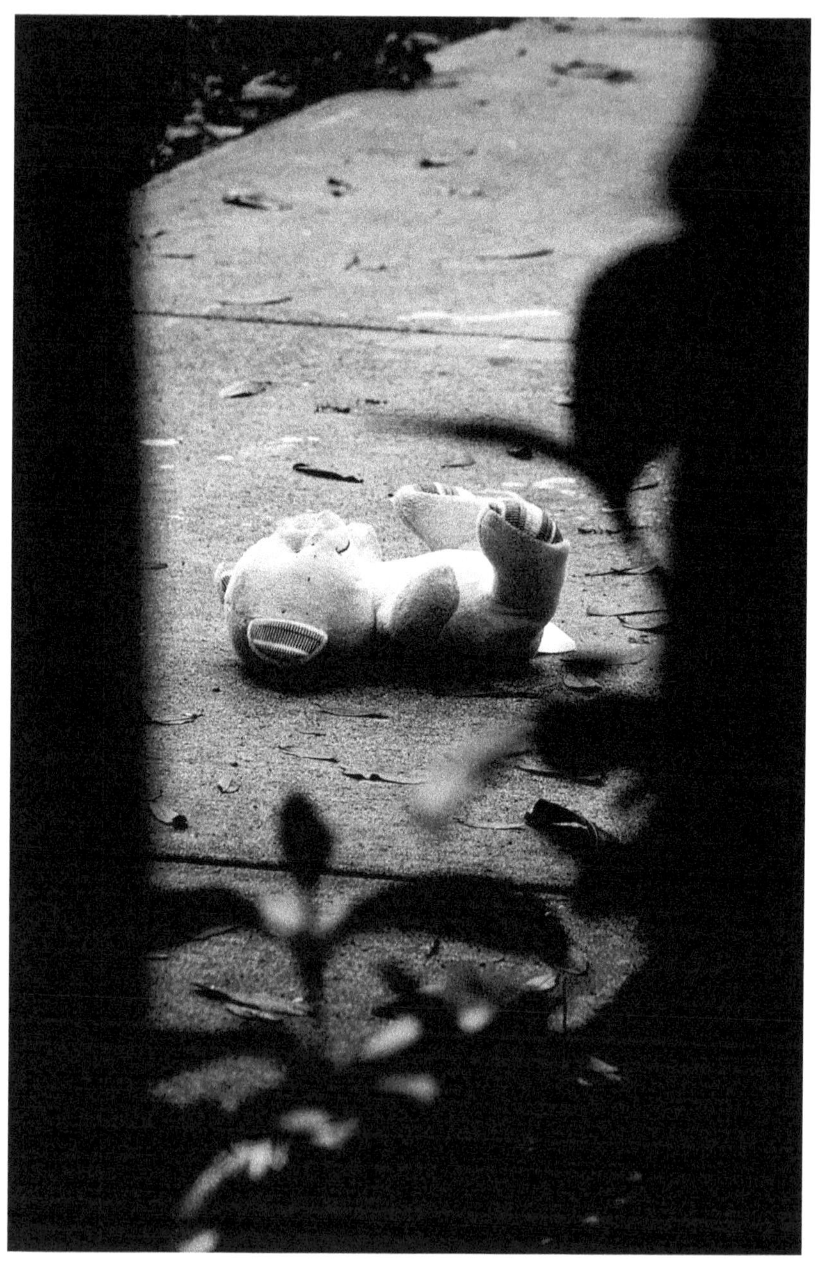

Holes

A best friend moved away
Dreary thoughts, dreary day
Hole in the soul like a missing tooth
Children never understand

A girlfriend's kiss gone astray
Dreary thoughts, dreary day
Hole in the soul like a full gut-kick
Youth seldom understands

A wife's cross words, emotions splay
Dreary thoughts, dreary day
Hole in the soul like a forgotten dream
Men rarely understand.

A child rebels in every way
Dreary thoughts, dreary day
Hole in the soul like a lost mint jewel
Fathers struggle to understand

A son or daughter abused at play
Dreary thoughts, dreary day
Hole in the soul like a hollow nail
Understanding fails to come

A life witnesses torture. Disgust. Dismay.
Dreary thoughts, dreary day
Hole in the soul like the absence of a mother's love
I will never understand.

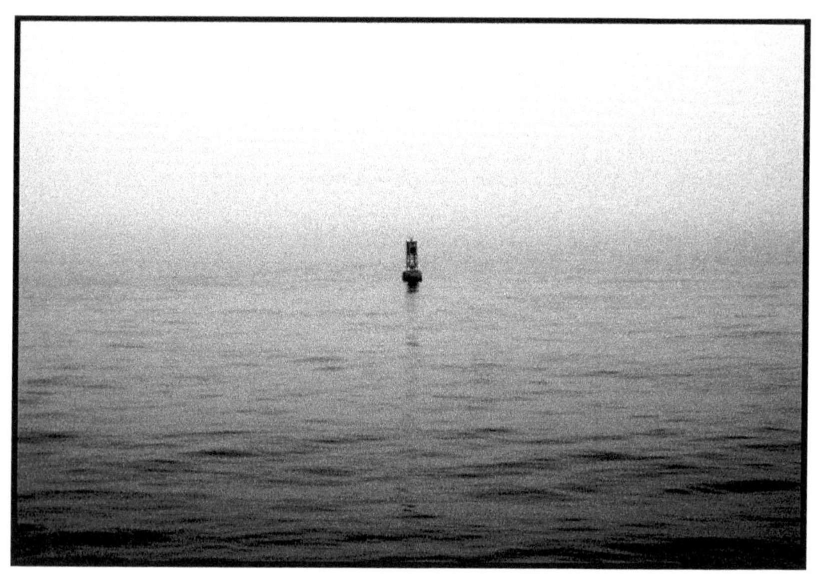

Gray Days

Gray days, wandered thoughts,
Wind tickled leaves, melancholy bought.
Ramshackle dreams, ideals on winds of change
Borne quiet to little islands – humanity deranged.

Islands of refuge and islands of hell,
Storms of indignation, apathy, sadness – oh well.
Life dug deep into the soul,
Sand islands die, engulfed by the whole.

Need, in many packages rushed,
Hunger, shelter, desire crushed.
Need delivered daily whether asked for or not
Efficient answers come only to naught.

Gray days, thoughts wandered, blue
Soul sunlight attempts to peek through
Landscapes littered by dreams now dead,
Islands covered, sandcastles awash in dread

Bridges built to kindred souls, they
Craft their castles just like you may
Wonder whether anyone hears
Love whispered through the years

New breath forged with each new day
Another dream to take away
Another soul to fly its course
Another death without remorse

We suffer this life, we strive for more
We fall and fail, become life's whore
Yet up we're lifted with each kind word
Heart engaged, heartbeat stirred.

One day we'll connect to other hands
Learn the ways of other lands
Learn to live together and die
Without questions as to why.

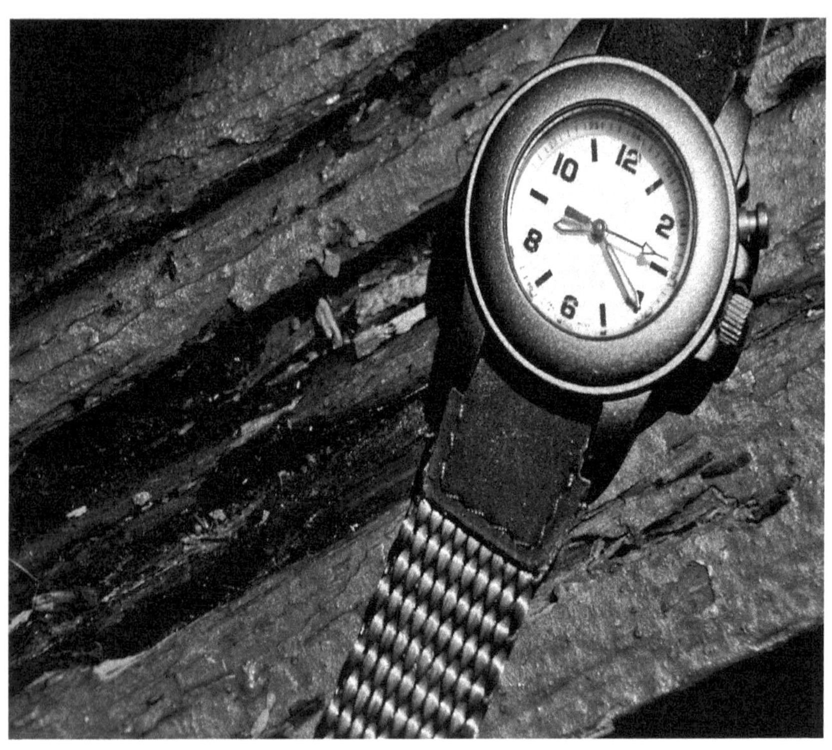

Time Share World

Each born in our time and space
Varied station, varied fate
Common existence on one little world
Life's fruition, lifetimes' unfurled.

Shared my time with Eisenhower,
Mary Tyler Moore and Tyrone Power
Apollo launched to see the moon
Hurricanes, blizzards, tornados, monsoons.

We share our time here, a true time-share resort
Amenities enhanced by our goodwill report
Checked off the day we draw our last breath
Our time-share world we own until death.

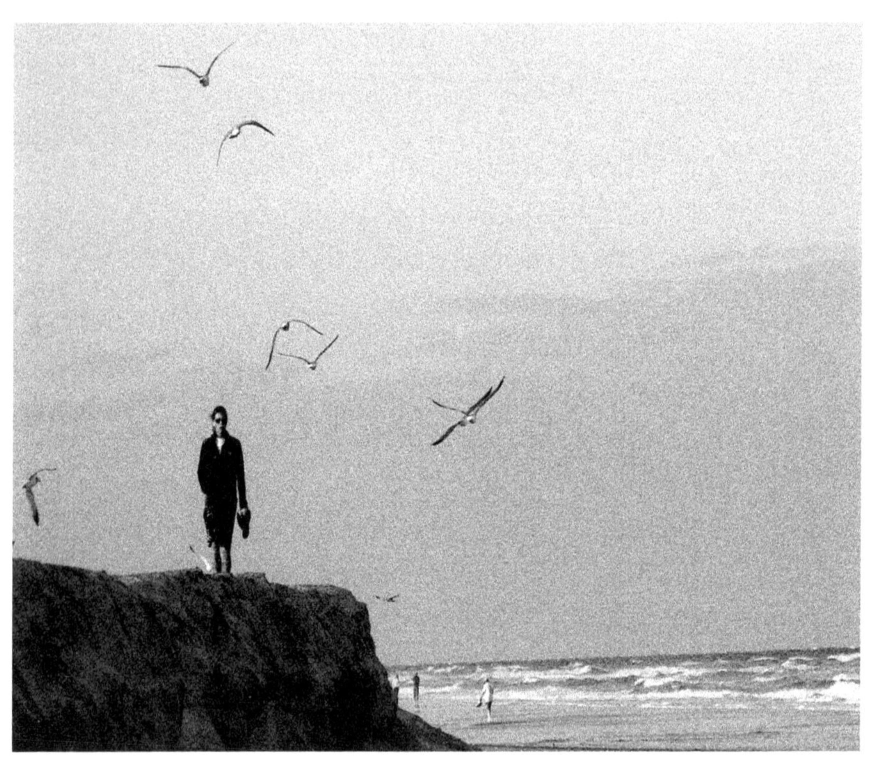

Golden Strand Smile

A golden strand smile
tickles her eyes, green and welcome,
a sign of mirth gurgling
beneath the soft rise and fall of her heart
as I continue to stumble over gangly words
in need of a good sanding,
not because they are sharp or unkind
but because the words come forth as damaged
and pained and solemn and mournful and sad and heart-broken
when all I want
is to capture that smile as ally,
not derogator,
so my own heart may rise and soar
and whisk the veil covering my desire away
and share breaths, conversations, ideas and
ideals until the golden strand smile turns
silver, familiar and cozy as a warm autumn day.

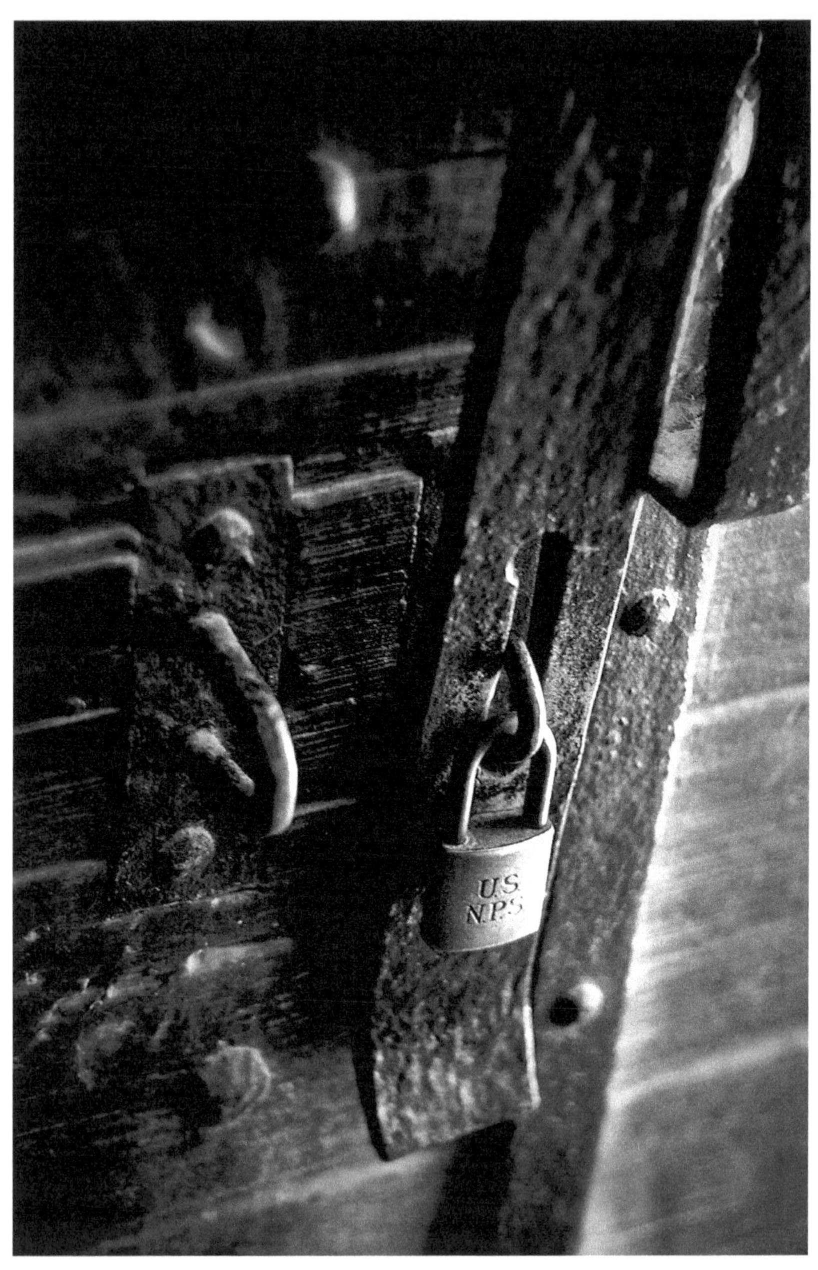
U.S.
N.P.S

Give Me Some Room

Monday morning hit me 'bout an hour ago,
Three in the afternoon, just a little slow.
Countin' down the time till I get out of here,
Get me through this rush hour traffic - get me to my beer.

Tuesday morning asks me to wake up on time,
Seems the work-week's nothing but an uphill climb.
When it all gets to me, and I really want to quit,
I push my work aside and I tell the world to shit.

Give me some room
Give me room to breathe.
I don't live my life for you
I live it for me.

When the world gets old and nasty, the work gets really slow,
When they have you in a stranglehold and they won't let you go,
Listen to what I'm saying, and make sure that you do it,
Stand back from it all and tell the world to screw it.

Give me some room
You've got to let me breathe.
You better give me some room
'Cause I'm beginning to seethe.

Give me some room
I'll be taking this no more
You'd better give me some room
Before I kick down the door.

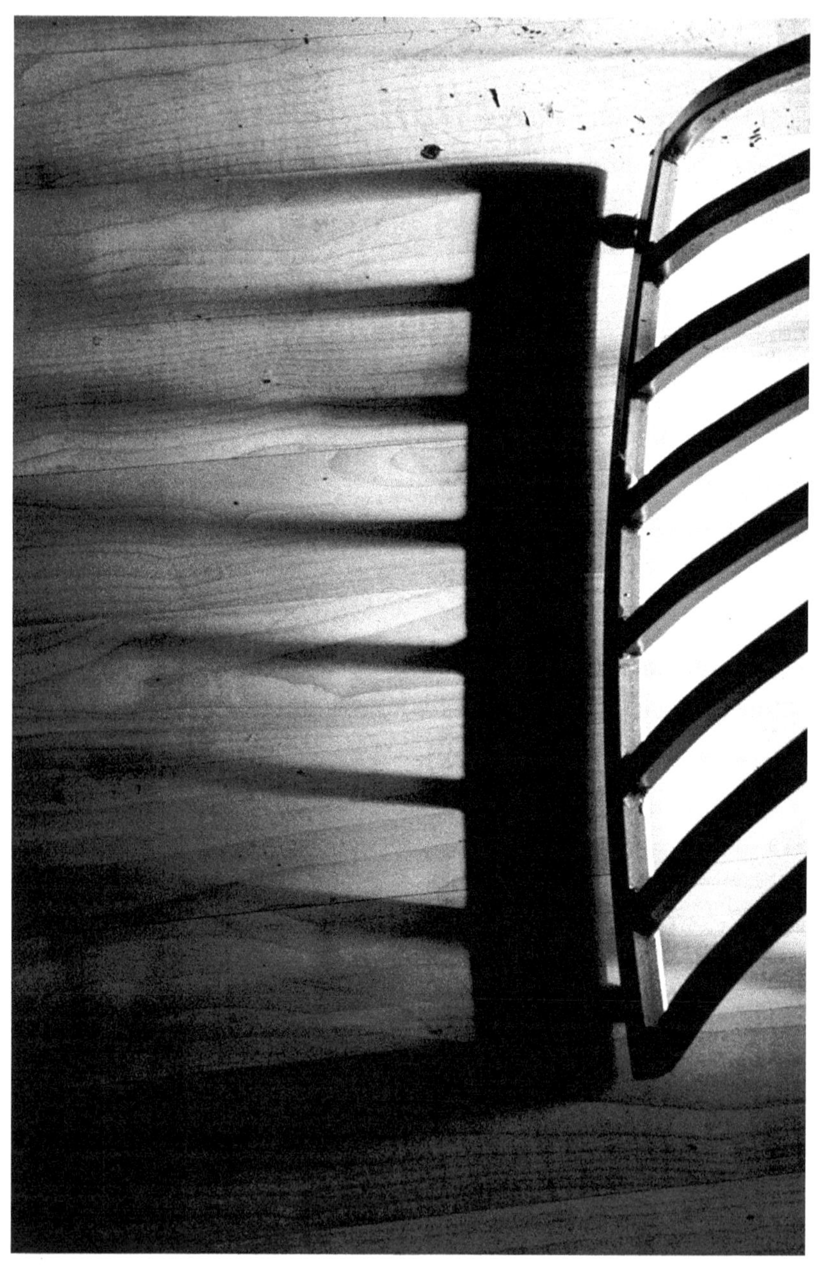

Eternity's Gaze

Eternity stares at me.
At once I am a meaningless speck of life
On an insignificant planet
In a confused solar system
Comprised of a pointless galaxy,
Eternity only has time to wink my direction before I expire.

Then, I am all the life and meaning in existence,
Commanding the only thought and knowledge from my inner perspective,
Unattainable in complete duplication anywhere in the total existence of Eternity.
A unique life.
An individual.
Yet, a meaningless fleck of lint on the shirtsleeves of perpetuity,
If only for that quick wink.
Does it really matter?

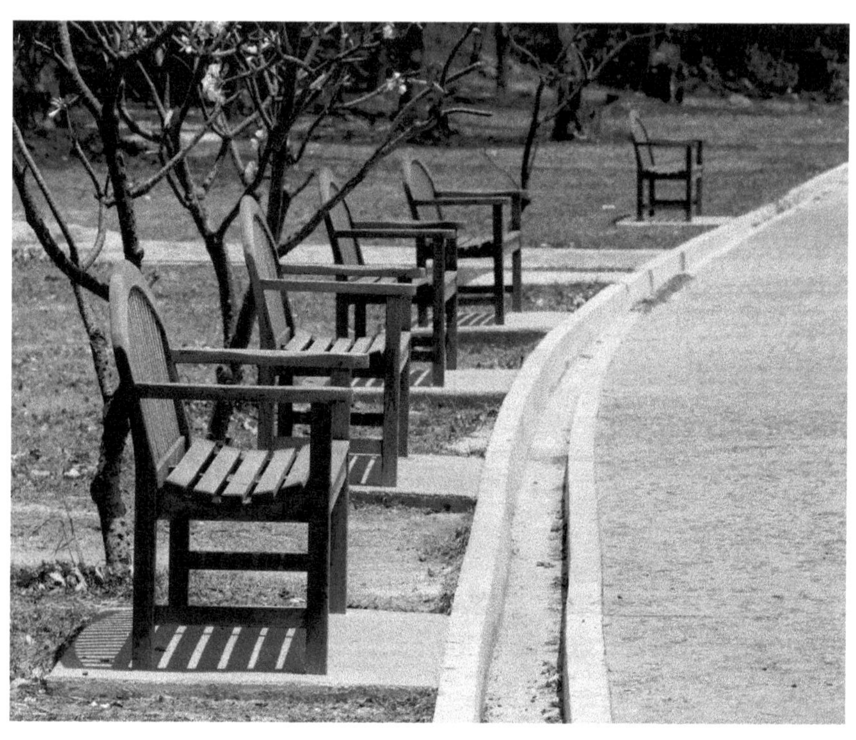

Delineation of a Shattered Heart

Pain impales synapses.
Sinus' overloaded on the brink of explosion.
From the hours of ground teeth?
Or the millions of tears withheld?

Gut riddled by knots.
That sick pre-puke feeling.
From the unanswered cries of a broken heart?
Or the persistent attack of a supposed ally?

Need trampled by disregard.
Love and empathy shattered.
Decades of abuse makes her so shallow and uncaring?
Or hatred and dogged reliance on battles her comfort?

Grace untouched by unwilling hands,
That need only employ its precepts.
Retched culmination of detonated formative years?
Or vicious refusal to adopt a perceived weakness?

My soul grieved.
Malevolent forces in adamant work mode.
Labor of self-perceived self-preservation?
Or weapon that cuts precisely through the core of my tenderness?

In this place of vows and oaths,
Alone with the stars, midnight moon, heat lightning,
Dare I step from these shadows of hopelessness?
Or testify to God and myself…
Surrender?

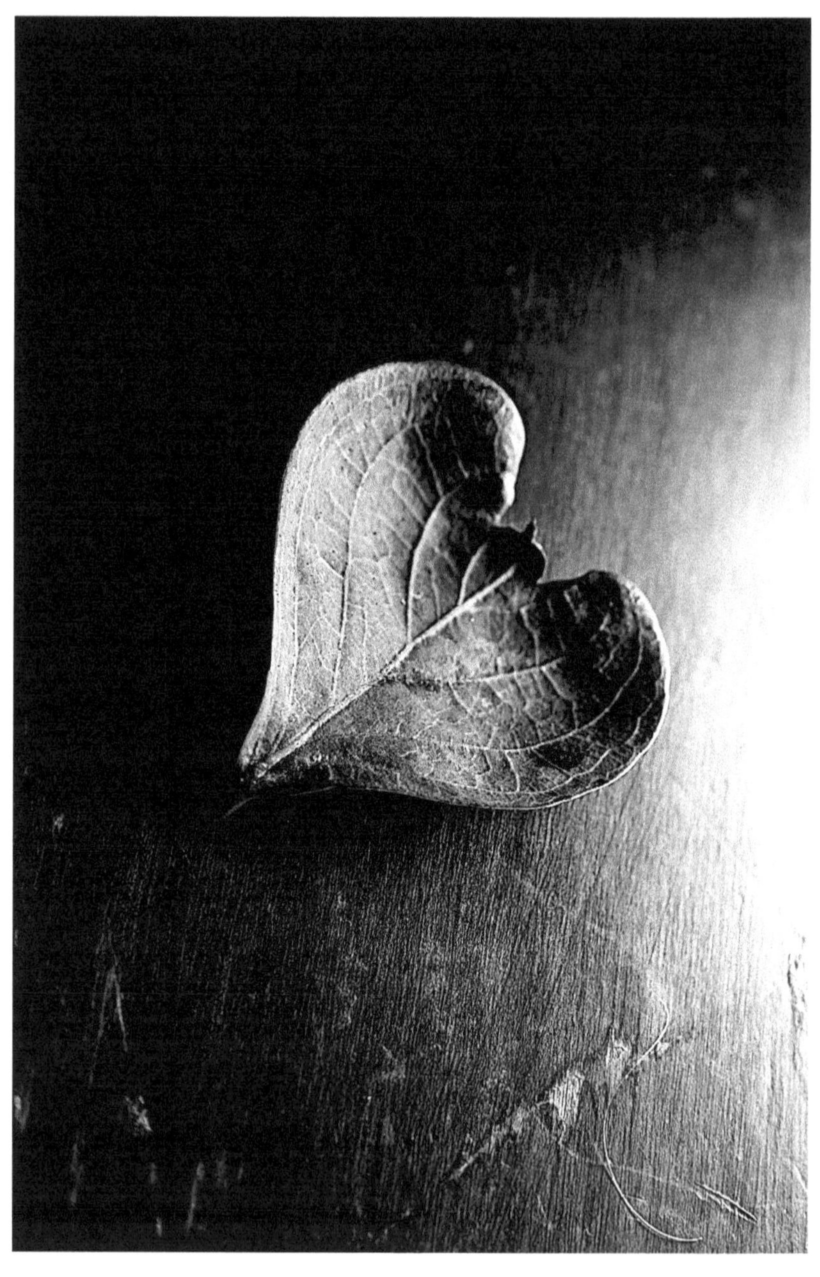

Dear Diary

Her heart

Prized above life

Beautiful each new day

Empathetic magnificence

She dominates my dreams, longings and soul,

My very breath rides within her

Our heartbeats share rhythm

My love desires

Her heart

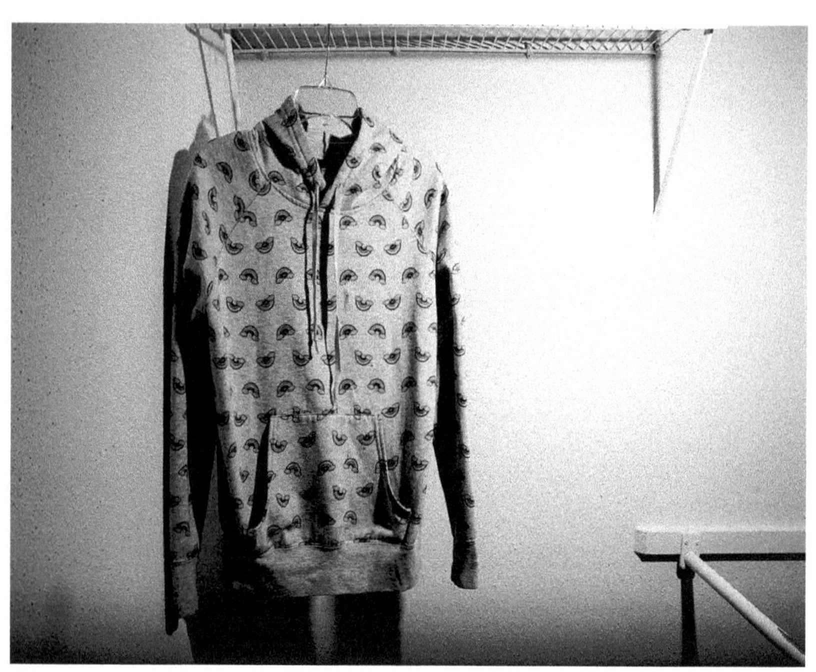

Crystalline Dream

A night sky twinkles - crystalline dream

Hushed floating patters - a landscape of cream

Fires banked high – dances of flame

Hot cocoa in hand – shivers to tame

December roars – yet beauty given

Soft boot crunches – white blanket driven

Inverted ice candles hung – sparkles in tow

Nothing more lovely – fresh fallen snow.

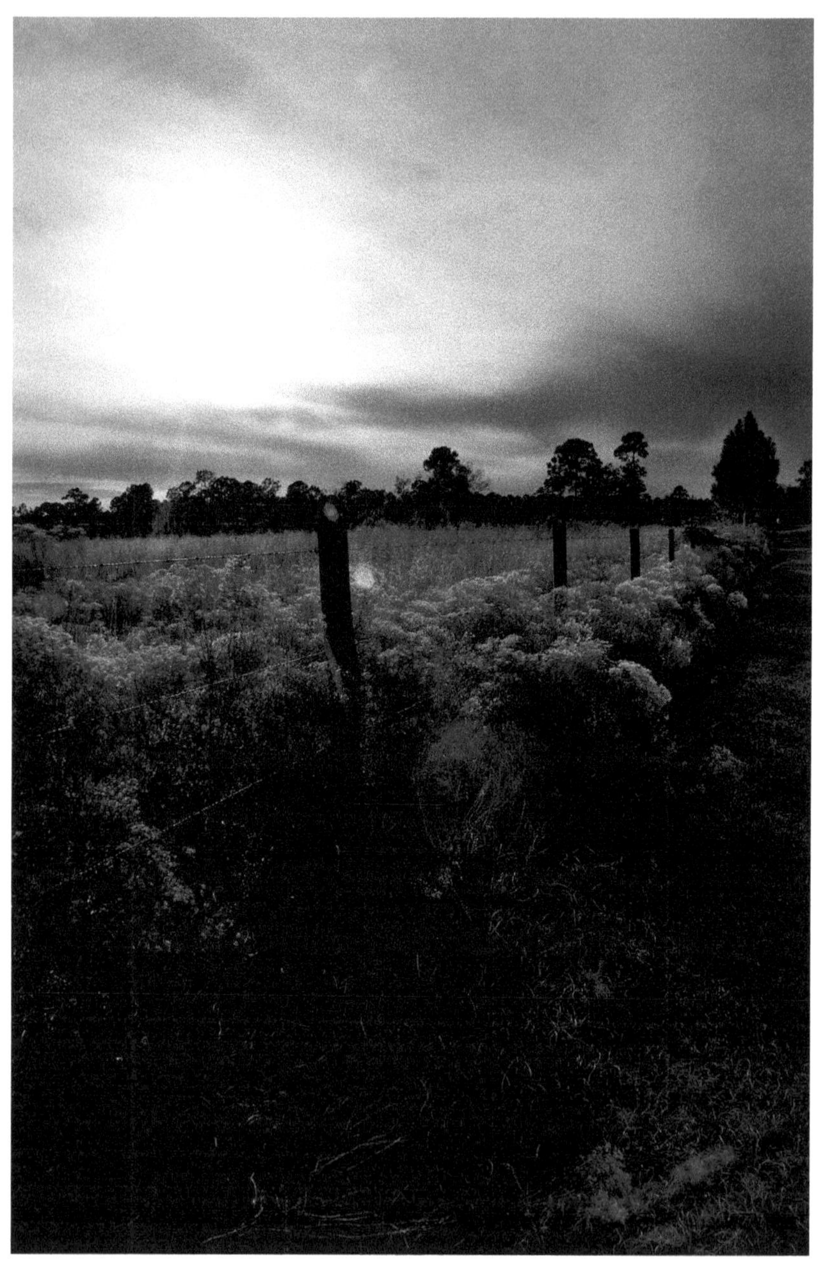

August Moon

Her voice of light crafts a song
Wisps and curls of gossamer clouds
Chorused by innumerable stars
Grandeur to the celestial horizon

Soft melodies hum the wind
She tickles imaginations
Leaves rustle, branches bend
Comfort for the dullest of hearts

She lends light to the lonely,
Frees captive souls from slumberless nights
Passes a free spirit through the essence of man as
Peace stands firm under this August Moon

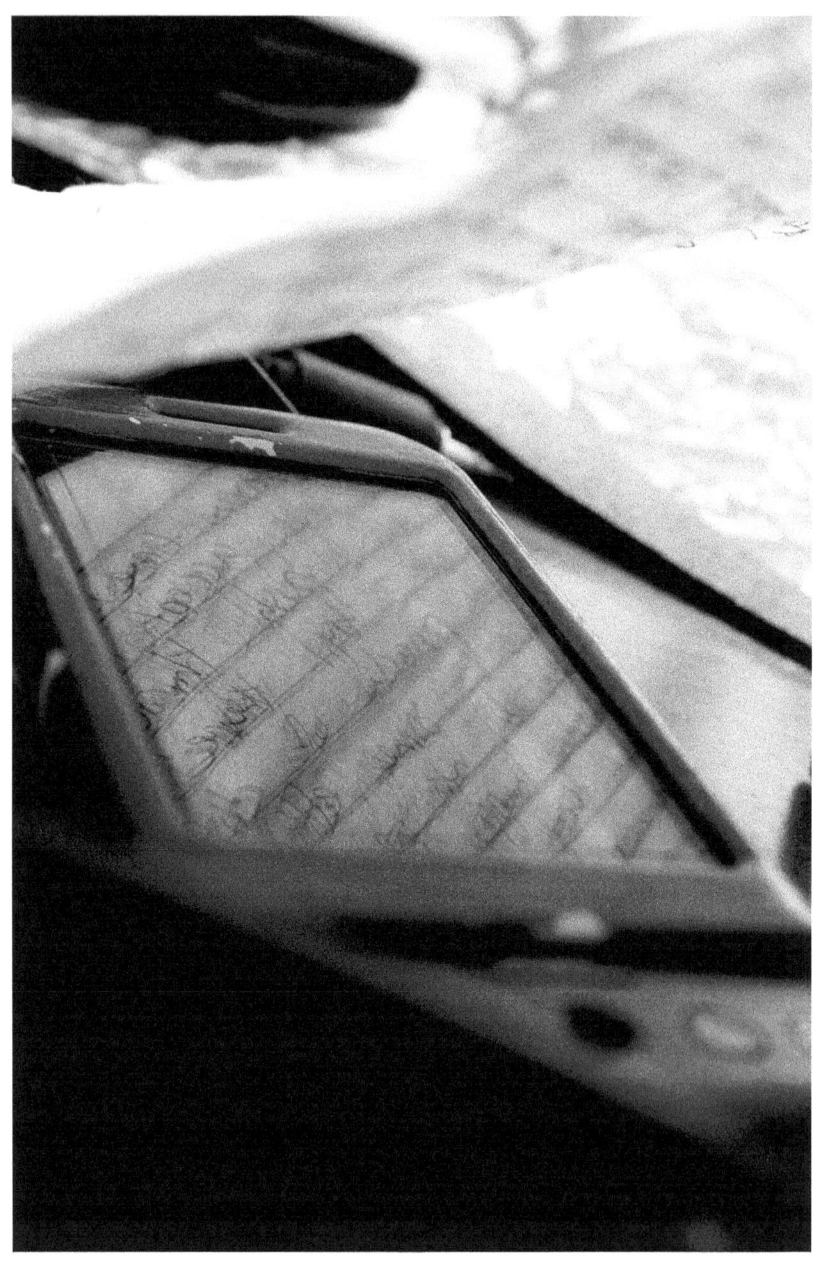

Anything Left to Give?

Books and words and songs ago
Life meant more than meaningless hours
Supplanted by humdrum days

Every breath an opportunity for love, romance
Every step, adventure driven
Every thought, idealistic and fresh
Every emotion available in force.

Now screens and sound bites and cacophony
Constrain the day from carefree whims
Gathered by fantasy's dreams.

Every breath a struggle for existence, survival
Every step, a labored trudge
Every thought, old and forlorn
Every emotion beaten down through time.

Will to move forward
Begs a question better served unanswered
Anything left to give?

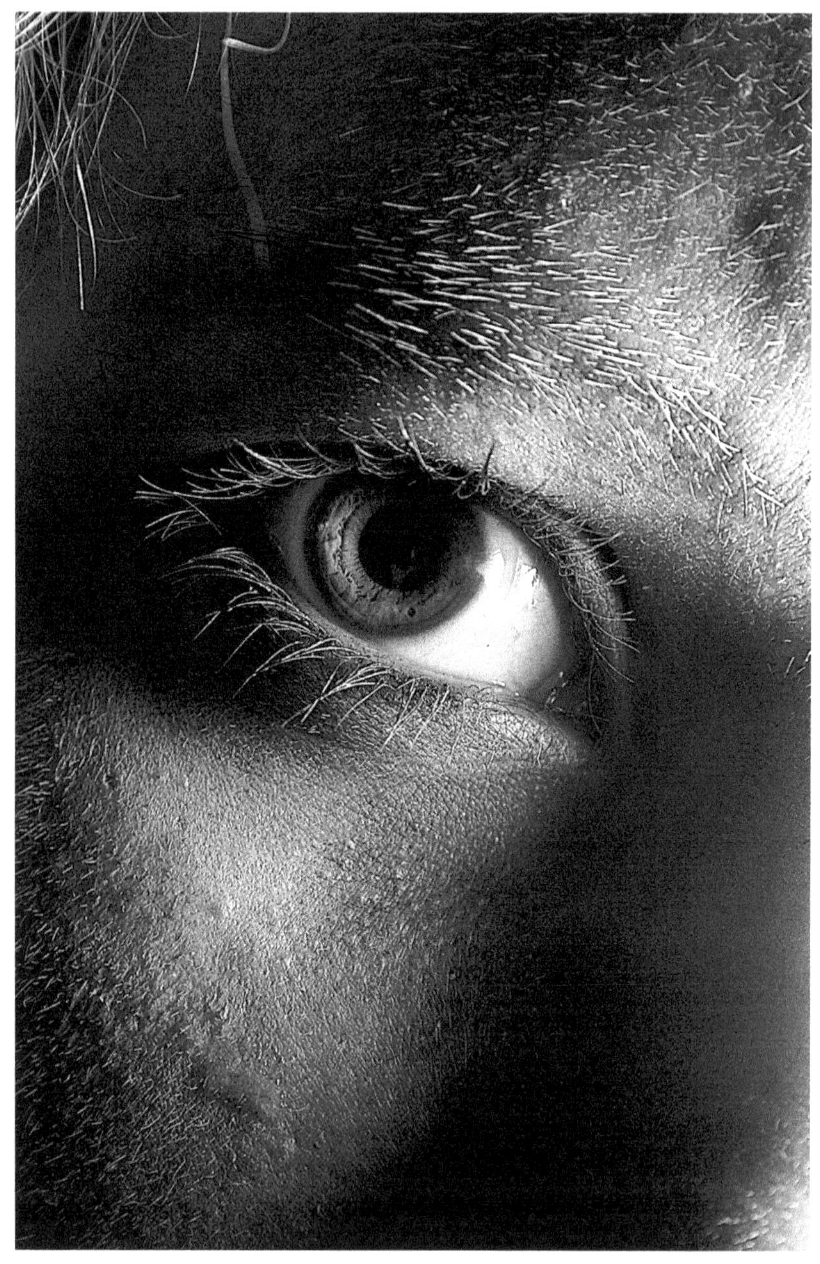

A Wonderful Life

Night breezes - gentle caresses,
Warm as a first kiss that blots out stars
Memorable as a rollercoaster that grips your heart
Tender as a tear of joy.

Sails - filled by soft whispers
Billowing into autumn years
Horizon the life and loves of a
Sunset absent of regret.

Faded light - gentle caresses
Memories of a heart gone wild
Smiles as ageless as countless
Tender as a tear of joy.

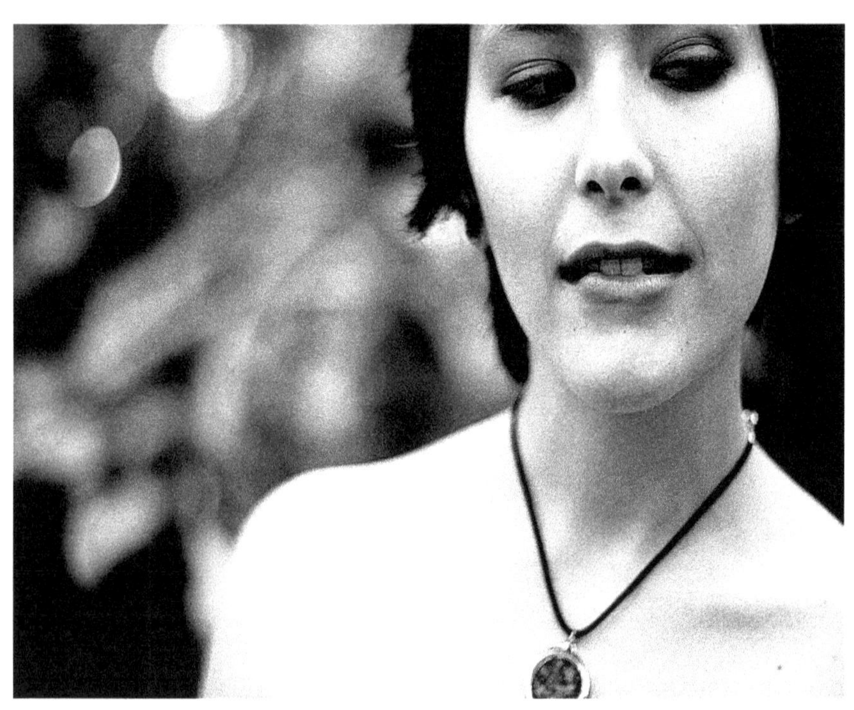

A Kiss Remembered

Moonlight magic, star sprinkled lake,

Her eyes, love's motivation, dreams folded in a moment's chance.

Lips soft as summer breezes, feathered in passion's nest,

Faint heart thrummed to life, a kiss slew this mortal's breath.

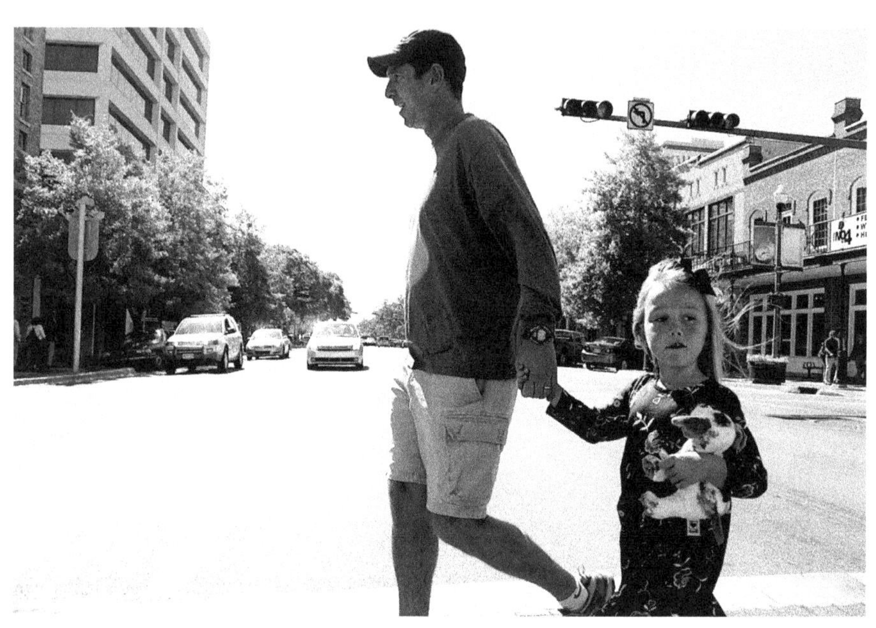

A Father's Tears

"A baby" clanks against recognition,
Foreign words. Joy. Elation.
Speculation, expectation,
A father's tears surge through smiles, hugs and kisses.

"It's a boy" puffs pride to his veins.
"It's a girl" softens his masculinity
Either chord snip
A saline stream for futures yet met.

Bicycle face-plants mortify,
Bloody bundle a pain of frustration and love,
Unable to heal the hurt
He begs heaven itself for substitution.

"I hate you," angry teenage words assail
Love beaten to his heart's very walls
Unable to find their answers
He suffers years of patience for relief

"I was raped" dismantles all senses,
Rage a useless vigor, revenge a hollow response
Restoration a fervent grovel
His tears heal nothing, yet flow forever.

Fractured sensibilities rain like molten lead
He struggles to ease their pain,
Realizes life's hateful Hyde remains ever-present
Dogged resolve, he dives into love's fragile hope.

Days and nights and walks and talks,
Commitment to this bone of his bone
Time and soul and love - their allies
Unknown strength carries his face

"You should have protected" the internal accusing finger.
Wails and pleadings and undoneness his private hell.
Escape from the pain unanswerable in his lifetime,
Stray moment haunts – ever susceptible to tears.

"I love you Dad" the only words that will ever matter.
Forgiveness for years of failures to protect
A lifetime of work to show the solid strength of love
A father's tears fall unnoticed by the world.

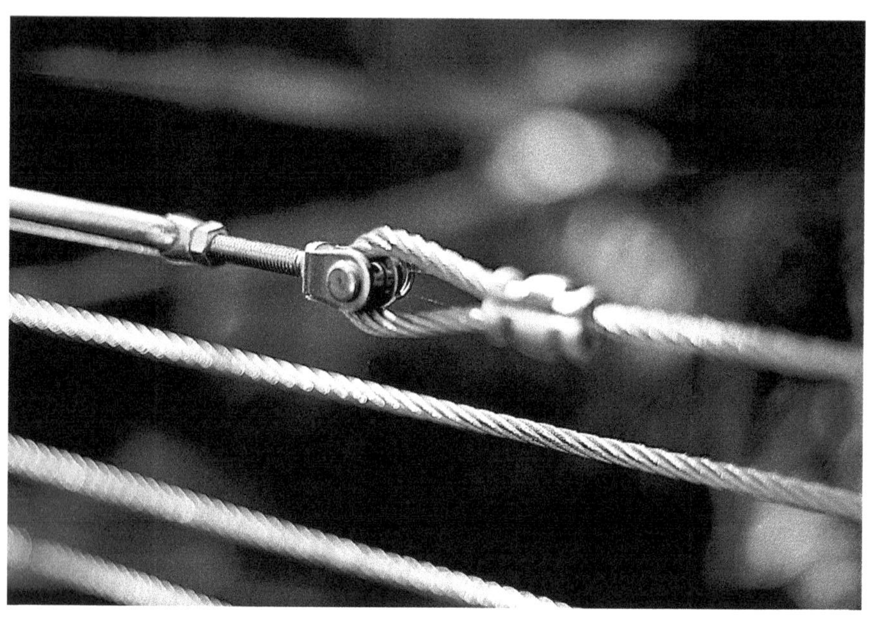

Writer's Soul

Passion. Passion stirs the writer's soul
Weaves cords of justice and mercy and love and hope
Drives this rope in whip-like fury at
Injustice and cruelty and hate and despondence.

Longing. Longing for connection to that voice we share
Weaves threads of tears and pain and sadness and misplaced ideals
Sews a tapestry of joy and healing and smiles and dreams
In an embroidery resplendent with the hues of life well spent.

Touch. Touch so gentle and fine, soft sliding silk that
Plays the length of our essence and spirit and character and heart
Suggests our core and courage and disposition and compassion
Can spring from the strokes of a pen or the lilting tap of modern keys.

A writer's soul cannot be dampened by
Mere catastrophe or pain nor damage nor sorrow
For these contain the fertile fields from which we breed our passions and
Rise up to the challenge of connecting… with inner peace.

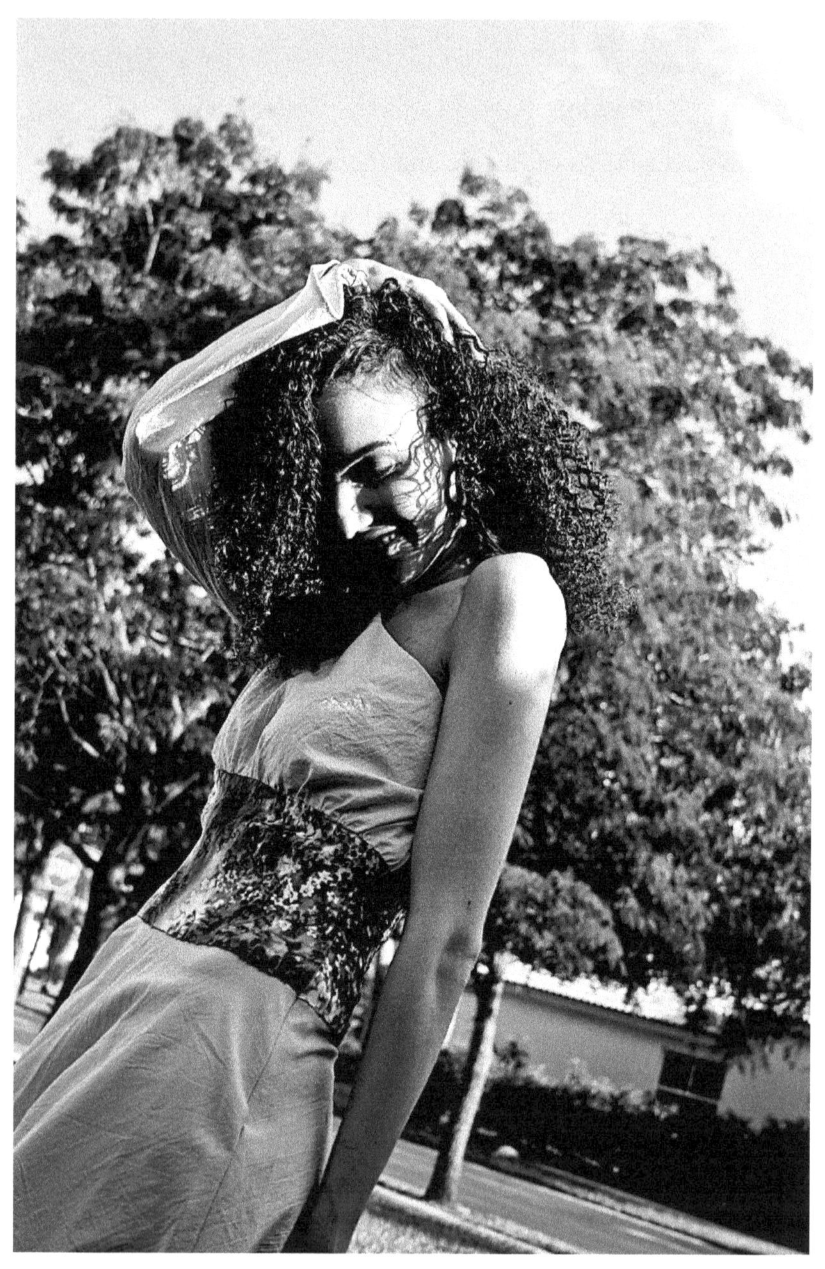

Twenty Minutes to Death

She sits there,
His lap full of her laughter.
She, spilling out of his arms.
Smiling, fawning porch nymph.

Pain stretches vile tentacles throughout my heart
Each word, each smile, each glance my direction,
Electronic cracks of tentacle whips against the fiber of my soul.
After 20 minutes she asks words of me,
"Say something."

Tears refuse their prescribed route,
"Something" tumbles off my tongue.
Like a grade school taunt gone horribly awry.
My back delivers the only goodbye I can muster.
My stiff, unwieldy retreat an unscheduled date with
life or death.

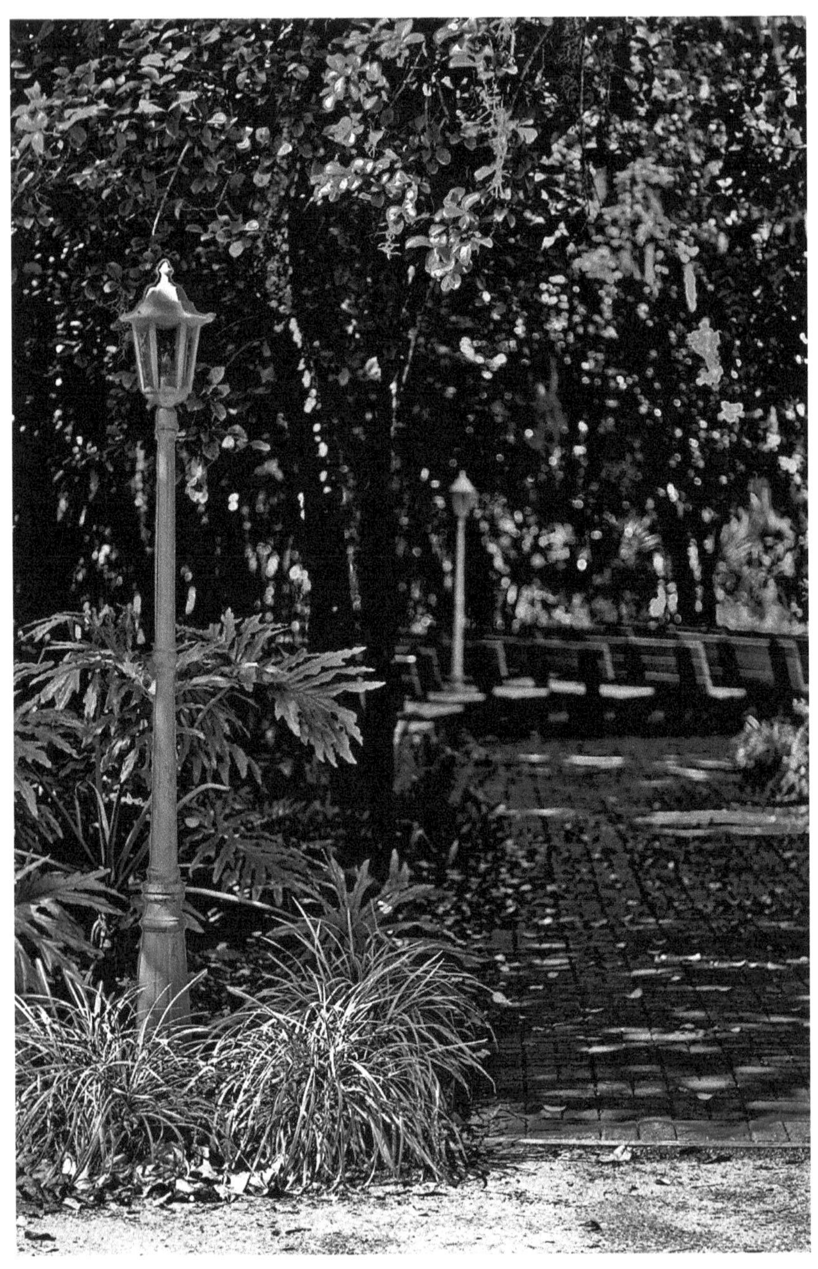

Blue Summer Song

Warm breezes brush through my hair
Full leaves clap with soft, gentle care
Summer tiptoes blue skies above me
Yet you are everything that I see

Clouds billow like silk candy fire
Heaven-bound hawks thermal higher and higher
Memories wander and ponder about you
Could you ever really think of me too?

Spring fell hard among the hot trees
Love followed - a dying cool breeze
I'm left here wondering what I will do
You are everything that I knew.

Wistful memories send me way back
My heart whispers of the love that I lack
Spring, cozy starlight, and wonderful you
Would turn my sadness to green from blue.

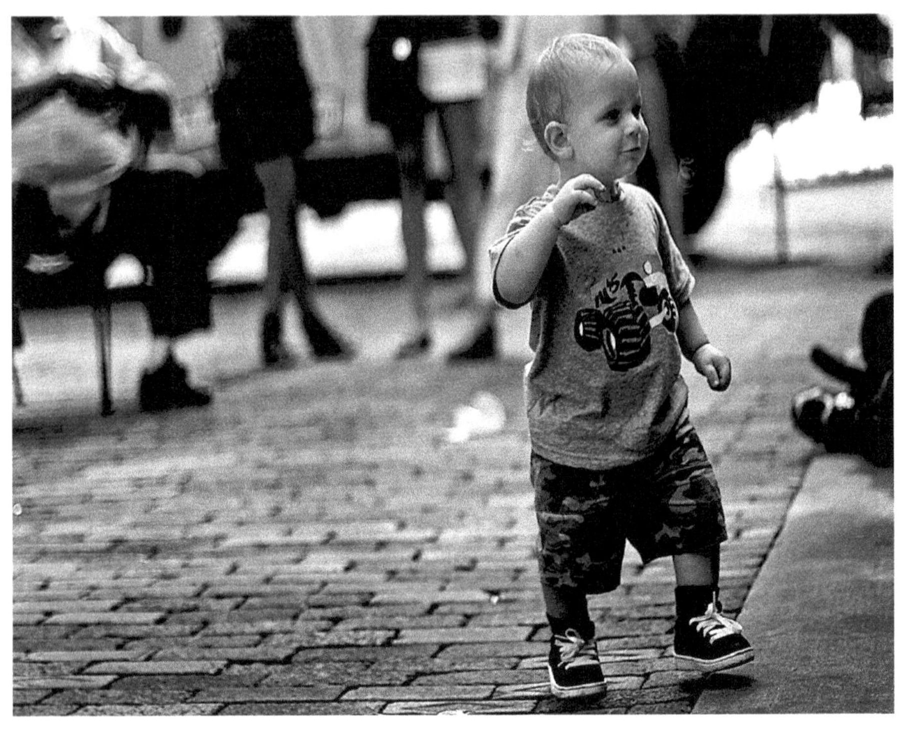

I Like it When...

...I hear my youngest daughter squeal, "Daddy! Daddy!" when I come home from work.

...I see my thirteen year old son make a big man's basketball move on the court.

...I get to hug my eleven year old daughter.

...I know peace comes to those who relax.

...People smile at me.

...I make kind eye contact with strangers.

...My wife is soft and loving.

...My teams wins.

...Autumn delivers scent-crisp air.

...I walk for the sake of walking.

...Music touches my soul.

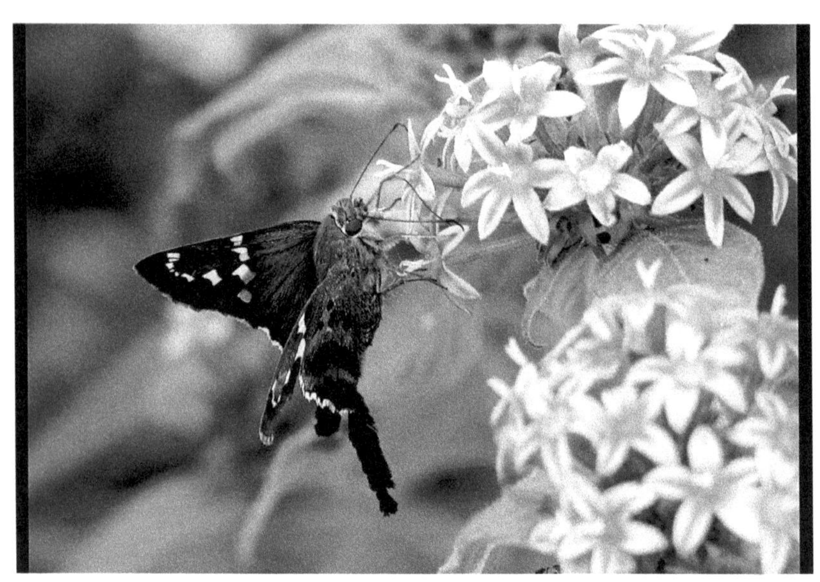

I Like it When … Part Two

…Moonbeams tickle snow shadows outside.

…Crystalline shapes mimic real-world existences.

…Hands run my sides and chest, and a hug breaks out around me.

…Smiles kiss my eyes, warm my heart and comfort my soul.

…Trains echo through mountain valleys with horns blaring their impending visit.

…Early afternoon shadows tumble from mountains onto sidewalks and roads.

…Cold autumn air snakes through my lungs and comes out as white-cloud ghosts on a breeze.

…My hand squirms into hers as we walk the riverbank home.

…The home of my youth welcomes me like I never left.

…Days and nights care for nothing but me and the one I love.

…My eyes drink in her hair, her walk, her quirks and her playful ways.

…I sit behind my keyboard and watch my life appear before me in symbols on the screen.

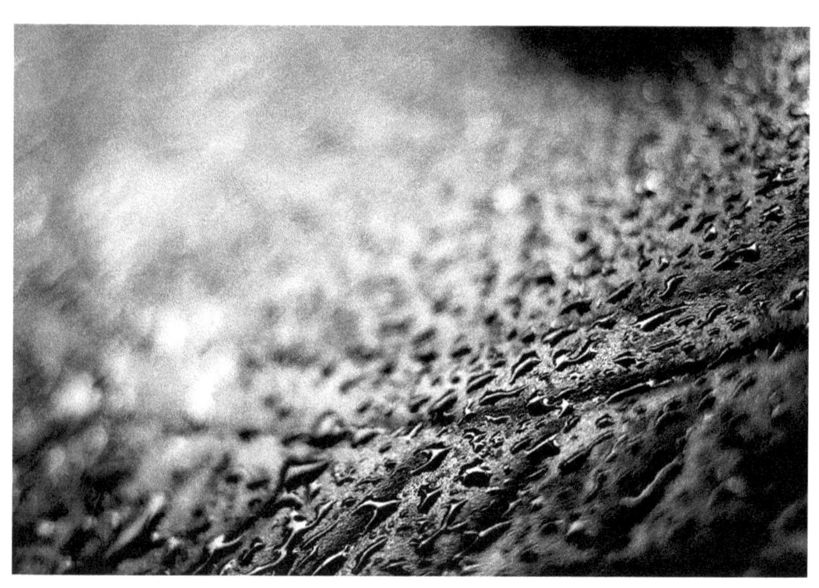

Limericks

The Enterprise was sure in a fix
Violent aliens disguised as sticks
Spock knew what to do
A large match he drew
And barbecued right there on the bricks

A prolific composer was Lizst
His music today may be missed
By a young eager crowd
Playing music too loud
Ignorant that eardrums he'd once distressed.

She swayed to the music on high
As she walked down the street with some guy
Who was oblivious to
The fact that she knew
Every man on the street's private sigh.

The limerick is dead one might say
Fallen from use in this day
Of poor rattled grammar
That pounds like a hammer
From tongues we would much rather spay

The kingpin sat forward his troops
The lynchpin was loosed for the loops
Of rope 'round the neck
Of a bird who bespecked
The clothespin's cache with loose poops

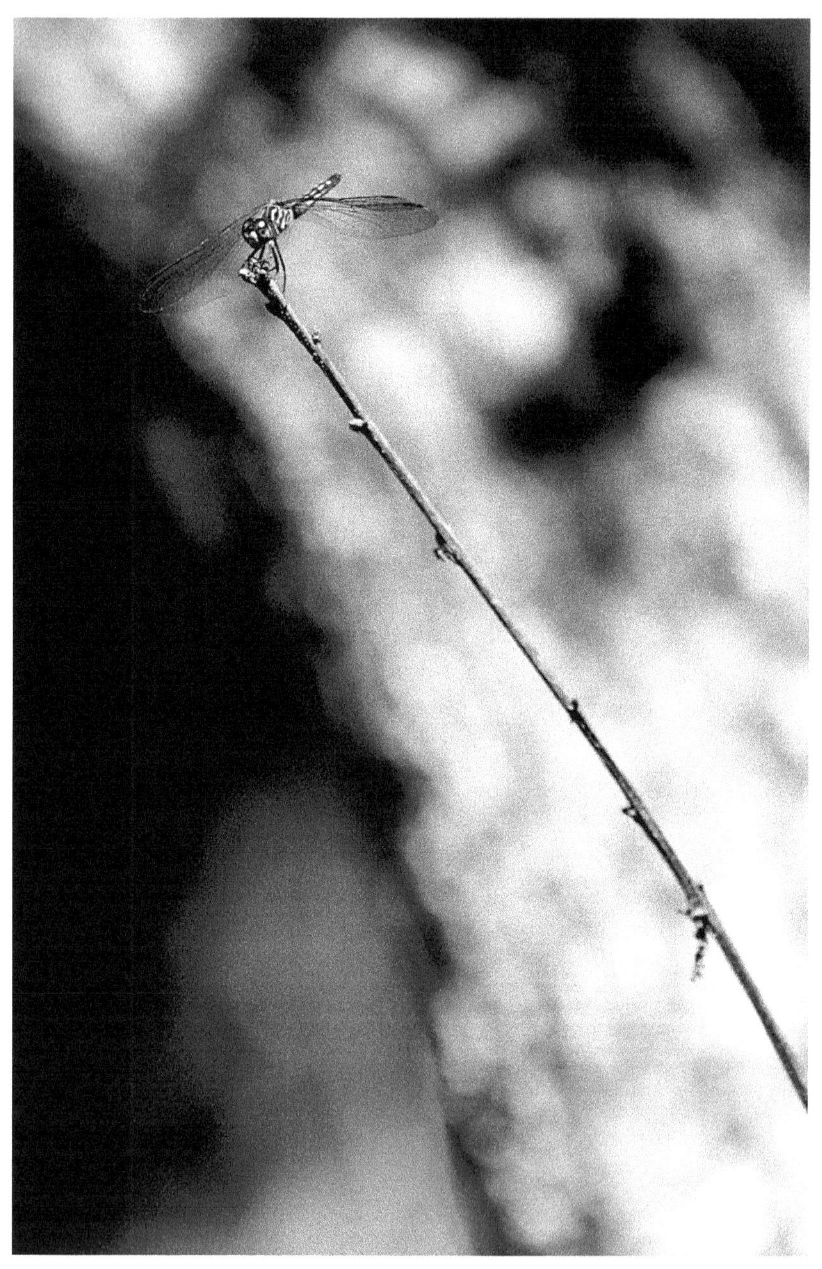

Limericks II

Maid Marian proceeded to suck
On a lemon provided by Tuck
The bitter taste riled
Her beauty defiled
By a face appeared struck by a truck

There once was a man from Nantucket
Whose wife would refuse to suck it
Until the orange came clean
In water from the stream
That he carried to the house in a bucket

Of sense and sensibility she would ponder
While he dallied hither and yonder
Until one day it seemed
She became really steamed
And he died so her heart could grow fonder.

Vile and wicked grew her rage and her pain
She searched for a kingdom to reign
Impervious to charms
They tied up her arms
Her condition they listed - insane.

Prolific at limericks was he
With children alongside his knee
He knew when to run
From a terrible pun
But he still had to try it, you see?

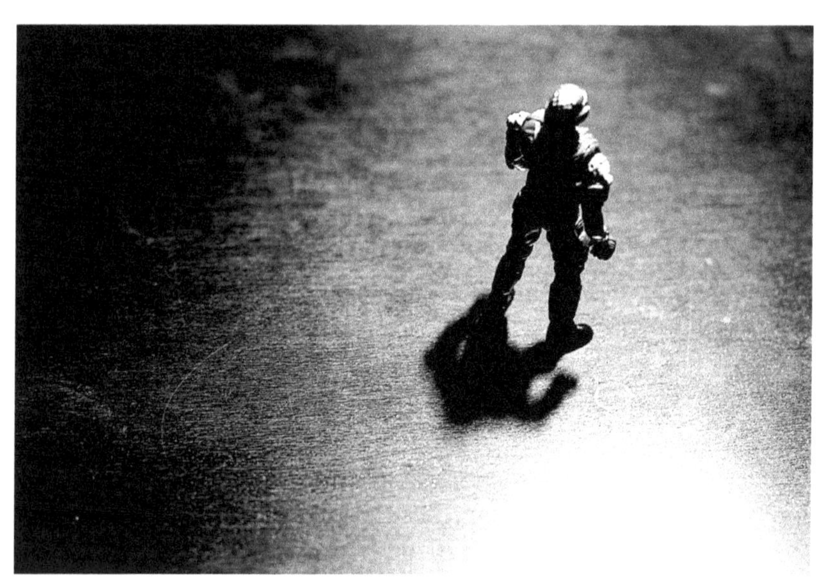

May 16, 1981

May 16, 1981

The day that died in infamy.

Day of graduation.

Day of intended marriage.

Day of last employment.

May 16 conjures relief.

May 16 remembers guilt and shame.

May 16 brings back panic and struggle.

May 16 should be removed from calendars everywhere.

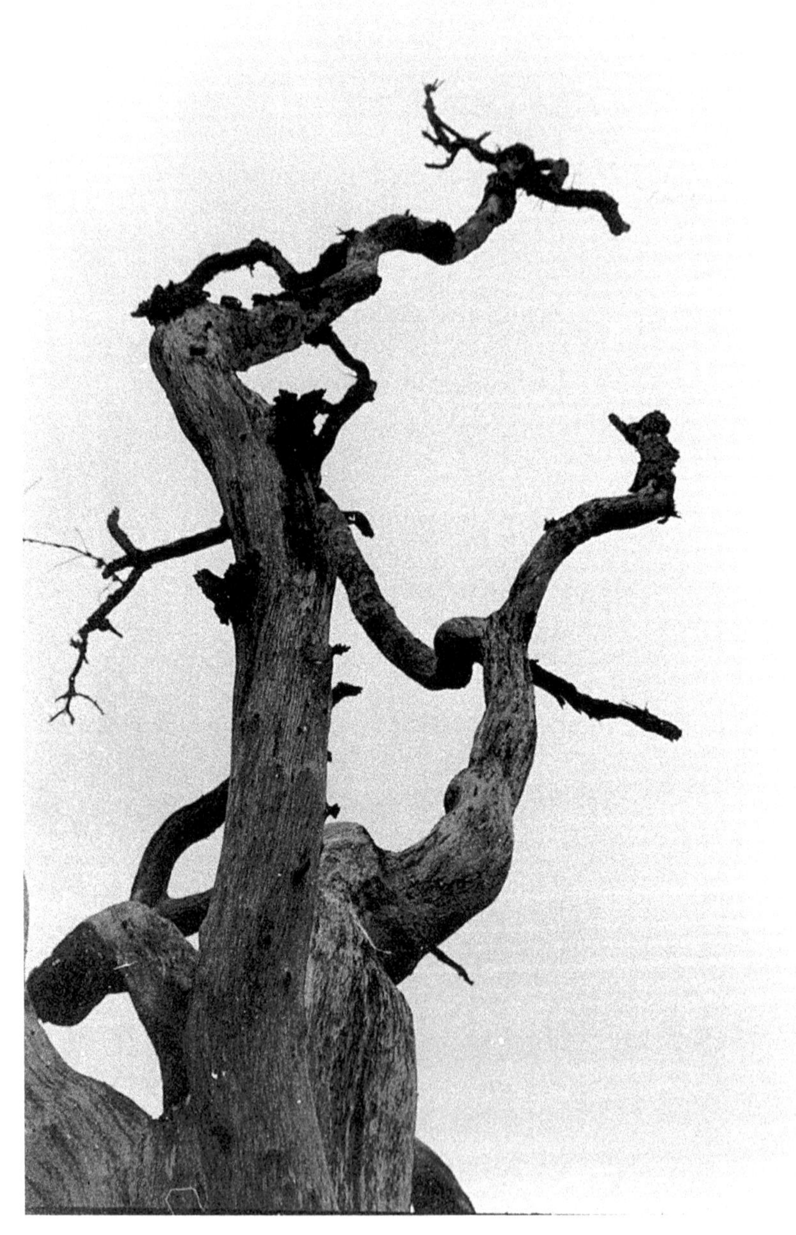

Memories and Time

Trees grey,

Sentinels to memories long locked away.

Deep golds, vibrant yellows, burgundies, reds

Memories die like autumn leaves

In cold, brittle cessations of life.

Ice fingers trail through heart byways,

Contemplations travelling to yesteryear.

Time wanders naked, trailing life's quirky lands,

Heeds no calls for slower pace.

Time lives on forever, a mocker of life.

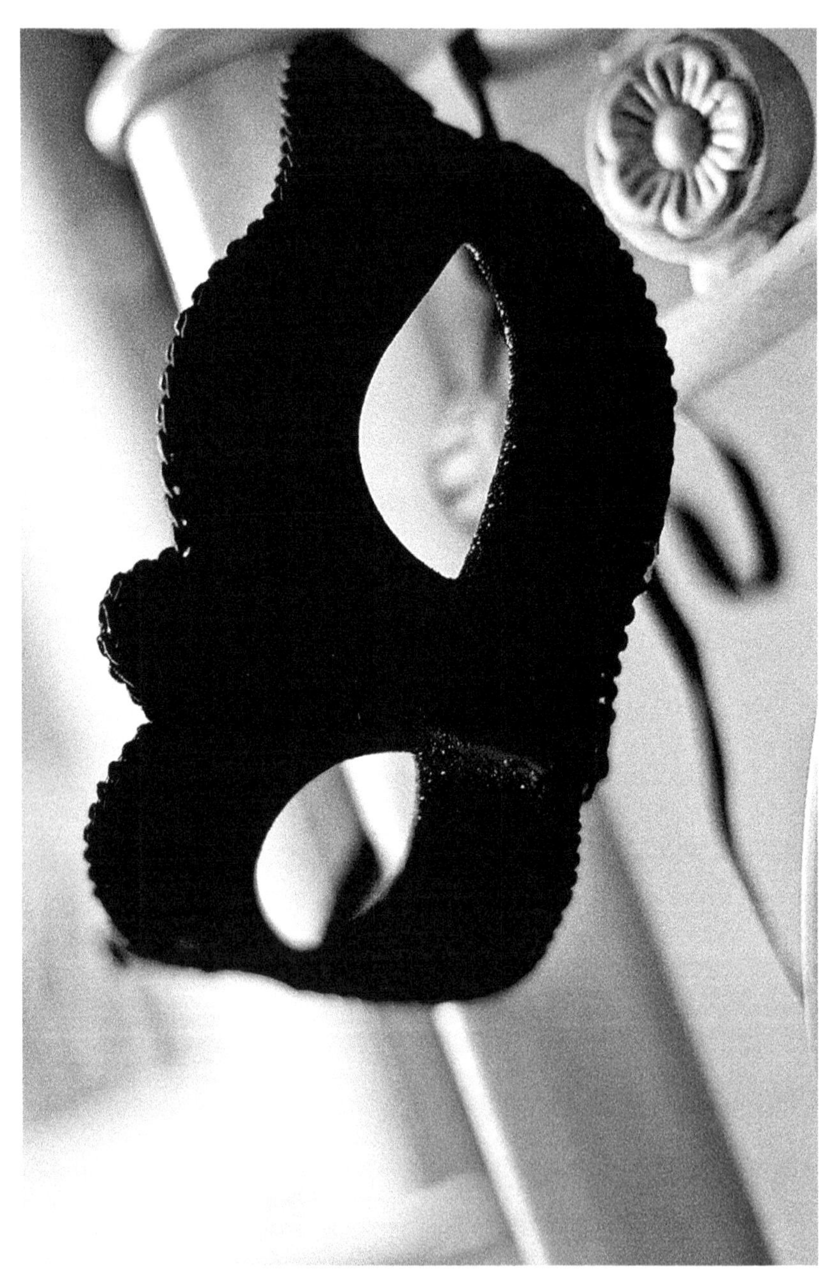

Play Me

Play me

Night whispers

Passions ripple the air

Fingertips to glide soft rhythms

On keys who beg to be used for pleasure

Play me

For I stand your ready lover

Who knows no remedy better placed

Than music and passion and love and peace

Always a medicine for melancholy.

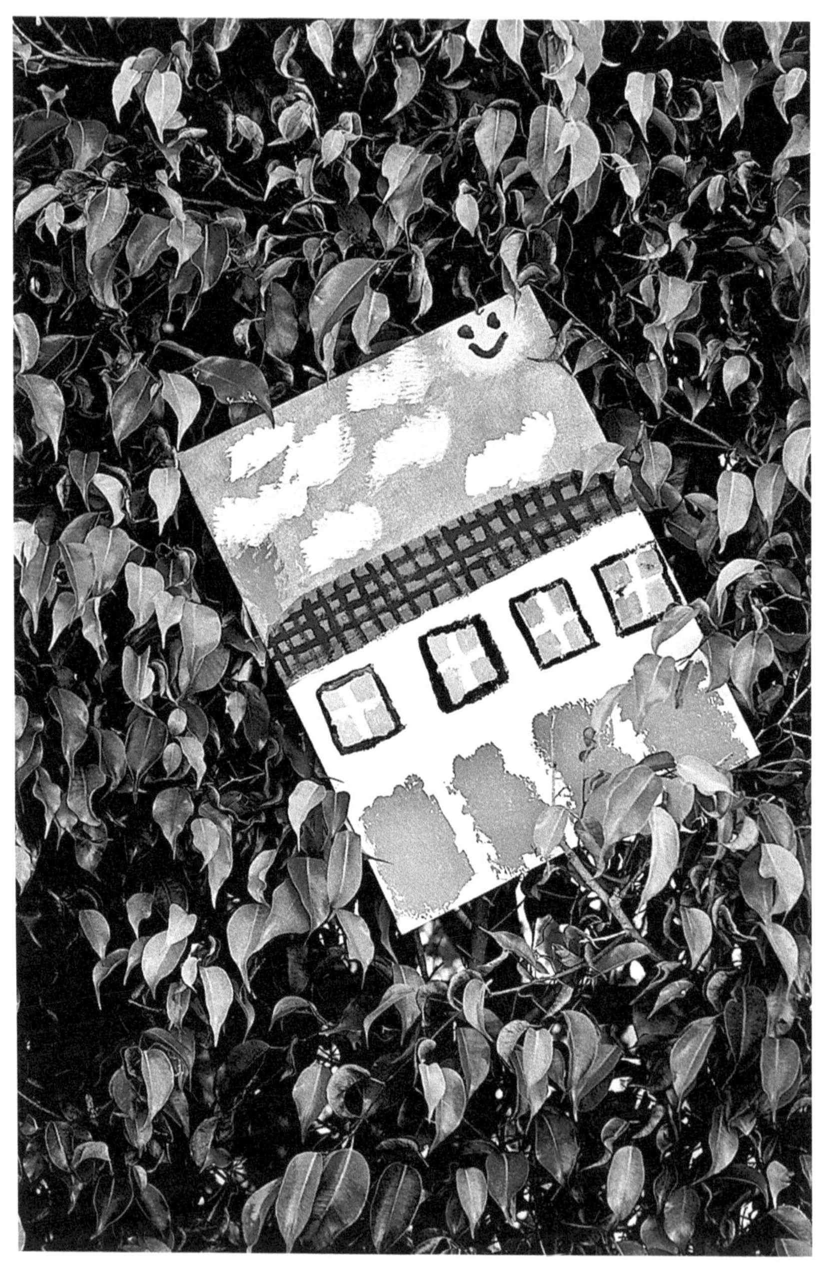

Skies

Lilting white clouds

Speckle horizons

Tickling the blues

And my mind

But my heart

desires

your focused attention…

Sigh

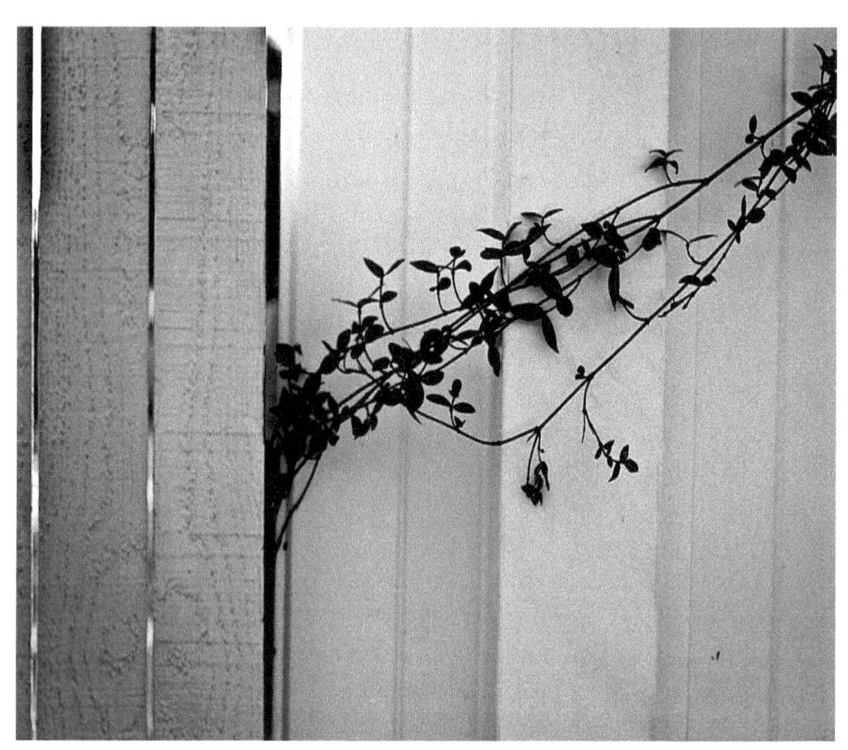

Summer's Song

Wind wending joyful summer leaves
Poet's ears tickled, poet's heart pleased
Fresh billowed clouds whisk away all pain
I'm living in the mountains again.

New start among rocks and streams
New beginnings for very old dreams
New vigor in these fingers of mine
Sing Summer's song of sweet, ready rhyme.

Years spent wandering this old earth
Beaches stole the home of my birth
Right from under my unthinking eye
Now I paint the mountain-backed skies.

New start among rocks and streams
New beginnings for very old dreams
New vigor in these fingers of mine
Sing Summer's song of sweet, ready rhyme.

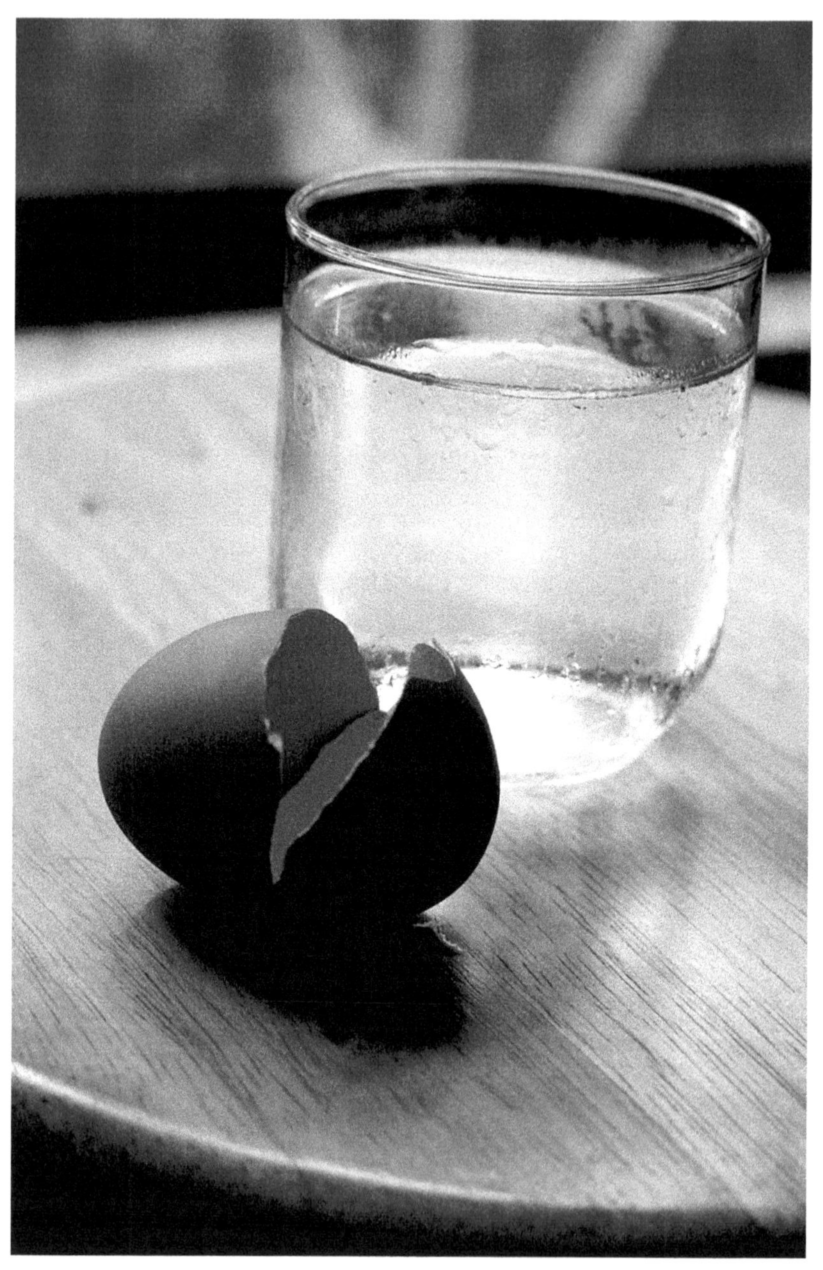

This Breath

This breath curls through my body
Proof positive life enjoys the moment
Not the future nor the past,
This instant of clarity and groundedness.

This breath reveals truth
Refreshing the cycle that carries the next moment
A stepping stone of comfort
The promise of future.

This breath contains everything I need
Hopes, dreams, passions
All I must do is acknowledge its importance
Use it in pursuit of that which I love.

This breath accompanies my life
From inception to death
Companion in dark places
Reveler in light.

This breath should be cherished no more, no less
Than the next that follows
Life wends its winsome trail throughout
Each and every breath taken.

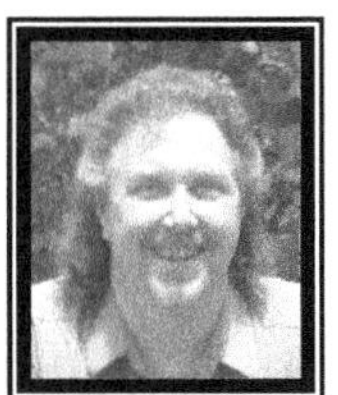

Michael Ray King is the author of the book - *Fatherhood 101: Bonding Tips for Building Loving Relationships,* a poetry book - *Loves Lost and Found* and this new collection, *Poetry in Black and White*. He and his wife Bobbie have six children and live in Palm Coast. Michael is president of ClearView Press Inc. a small press based in Palm Coast, and a former president of Coastmasters, the local Toastmasters club in Palm Coast. He also co-leads the Palm Coast FWA (Florida Writers Association) Chapter and is currently working on a joint novel project, *The Method Writers*, with his focus writer's group, the Rogues Gallery Writers. Michael has won five Royal Palm Literary Awards, three in the poetry category for poems from the book *Loves Lost and Found*, one for his book *Fatherhood 101* and one for his unpublished short story *Why Me?*.

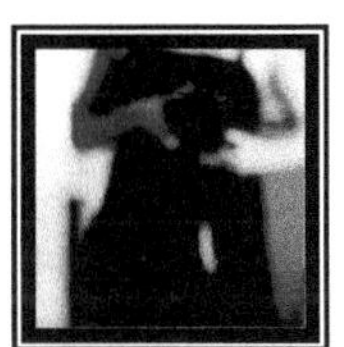

Ella Forrest was born the first day of spring in 1989 in New Jersey. She received her first camera at the age of five during Christmas morning. Little did she know that the Fisher Price camera would later influence her love of photography and how she observes her surroundings. Throughout her life she would often find these forgotten and miscellaneous items, then save them to the side feeling as though they were precious. This routine still exists in her life today, but now she also photographs those obscure objects. It wasn't until college that Ella developed her technical skills and enhanced her artistic abilities. Inspirational moments can come from mundane life experiences such as staring at the clouds and living with her two crazy cats. Currently Ella lives in St. Augustine and enjoys photographing anything from candid moments to commercial products.